PROBLEM-BASED LEARNING

CASE STUDIES, EXPERIENCE AND PRACTICE

D0061323

EDITED BY

PETER SCHWARTZ, STEWART MENNIN AND GRAHAM WEBB

CASE STUDIES OF TEACHING IN HIGHER EDUCATION

KOGAN PAGE

First published in 2001 by Kogan Page Limited

Kogan Page Limited
120 Pentonville Road
London N1 9JN
UK

Stylus Publishing Inc.
22883 Quicksilver Drive
Sterling
VA 20166–2012
USA

British Library Cataloguing in Publication Data

A CIP record for this book is available from the British Library.

ISBN 0 7494 3492 9 (paperback)
ISBN 0 7494 3530 5 (hardback)

Typeset by Saxon Graphics Ltd, Derby
Printed and bound by Creative Print and Design (Wales) Ebbw Vale

CONTENTS

Contributors

Deborah E Allen is in the Department of Biological Sciences at the University of Delaware, Newark, DE, USA (e-mail: deallen@udel.edu).

Emyr W Benbow is Senior Lecturer in Pathology at the University of Manchester, UK (e-mail: ebenbow@fs1.scg.man.ac.uk).

Amy V Blue is Assistant Dean for Curriculum and Evaluation at the Medical University of South Carolina, Charleston, SC, USA (email: blueav@musc.edu).

Martha G Camp is Professor of Medical Education at the University of Texas Medical Branch, Galveston, TX, USA (e-mail: mgcamp@utmb.edu).

John F Chaves is Professor in the Department of Oral Biology at the Indiana University School of Dentistry, Indianapolis, IN, USA (e-mail: jchaves@iupui.edu).

D Christopher Clark is Professor in the Division of Community and Preventive Dentistry at the University of British Columbia, Vancouver, BC, Canada (e-mail: dcc@interchange.ubc.ca).

Carol-Ann Courneya is Associate Professor of Physiology at the University of British Columbia, Vancouver, BC, Canada (e-mail: caotter@interchange.ubc.ca).

Rob Cowdroy is Head of the Department of Architecture at the University of Newcastle, Callaghan, NSW, Australia (e-mail: arrmc@cc.newcastle.edu.au).

Diana H J M Dolmans is Assistant Professor in the Department of Educational Development and Research at the University of Maastricht, The Netherlands (e-mail: D.Dolmans@educ.unimaas.nl).

Barbara J Duch is in the Mathematics and Science Education Resource Center at the University of Delaware, Newark, DE, USA (e-mail: bduch@udel.edu).

Elizabeth Ann Farmer is Associate Professor in the Department of General Practice at Flinders University, Adelaide, SA, Australia (e-mail: liz.farmer@flinders.edu.au).

Alan Fincham is Professor, Basic Sciences at the University of Southern California School of Dentistry, Los Angeles, CA, USA (e-mail: contact Charles Shuler).

Alex Forrest is Lecturer in Oral Biology at the University of Queensland, St Lucia, QLD, Australia (e-mail: a.forrest@mailbox.uq.edu.au).

Bren Gannon is Associate Professor in the Department of Anatomy and Histology at Flinders University, Adelaide, SA, Australia (e-mail: Bren.Gannon@flinders.edu.au).

Gordon M Greene is Associate Director, Office of Medical Education at the John A Burns School of Medicine, University of Hawaii, Honolulu, HI, USA (e-mail: greeneg@jabsom.biomed.hawaii.edu).

Susan E Groh is in the Department of Chemistry and Biochemistry at the University of Delaware, Newark, DE, USA (e-mail: sgroh@udel.edu).

David M Kaufman is Professor and Director of Faculty Development in the Division of Medical Education at Dalhousie University, Halifax, Nova Scotia, Canada (e-mail: david.kaufman@dal.ca).

Marilyn S Lantz is Professor in the Department of Oral Biology at the Indiana University School of Dentistry, Indianapolis, IN, USA (e-mail: contact John Chaves).

Marlene A Lindberg is Coordinator, Program Evaluation and Educational Research in the Office of Medical Education at the John A Burns School of Medicine, University of Hawaii, Honolulu, HI, USA (e-mail: lindberg@hawaii.edu).

Jan Lovie-Kitchin is Associate Professor at the School of Optometry, Queensland University of Technology, Kelvin Grove, QLD, Australia (e-mail: j.lovie-kitchin@qut.edu.au).

Raymond F T McMahon is Senior Lecturer in Pathology at the University of Manchester, UK (e-mail: Ray.McMahon@fs1.scg.man.ac.uk).

Barry Maitland is Dean, Faculty of Architecture, Building and Design, at the University of Newcastle, Callaghan, NSW, Australia (e-mail: contact Rob Cowdroy).

Karen V Mann is Professor and Director, Division of Medical Education at Dalhousie University, Halifax, Nova Scotia, Canada (e-mail: karen.mann@dal.ca).

Stewart P Mennin is Assistant Dean, Educational Development and Research, and Professor, Department of Cell Biology and Physiology, at the University of New Mexico School of Medicine, Albuquerque, NM, USA (e-mail: smennin@salud.unm.edu).

Barbara Miflin is Education Officer at the School of Medicine, University of Queensland, Herston, QLD, Australia (e-mail: b.miflin@mailbox.uq.edu.au).

David Price is Senior Lecturer, Academic Staff Development at the School of Medicine, University of Queensland, Herston, QLD, Australia (e-mail: d.price@mailbox.uq.edu.au).

David Prideaux is Professor of Medical Education at Flinders University, Adelaide, SA, Australia (e-mail: David.Prideaux@flinders.edu.au).

Isobel Rolfe is in the Dean's Unit, Faculty of Medicine and Health Sciences at the University of Newcastle, Callaghan, NSW, Australia (e-mail: rolfe@mail.newcastle.edu.au).

Sue Runciman is in the Department of Anatomy and Histology at Flinders University, Adelaide, SA, Australia (e-mail: Sue.Runciman@flinders.edu.au).

Nina Felice Schor is Professor of Pediatrics, Neurology, and Pharmacology at the University of Pittsburgh, Pittsburgh, PA, USA (e-mail: nfschor@pitt.edu).

Peter L Schwartz is Associate Professor in Pathology at the University of Otago Medical School, Dunedin, New Zealand (e-mail: peter.schwartz@stonebow.otago.ac.nz).

Ann Sefton is Associate Dean (Curriculum) in the Faculties of Medicine and Dentistry at the University of Sydney, NSW, Australia (e-mail: anns@gmp.usyd.edu.au).

Charles F Shuler is Professor of Craniofacial Molecular Biology at the University of Southern California School of Dentistry, Los Angeles, CA, USA (e-mail: shuler@hsc.usc.edu).

David Taylor is Director of PBL and Senior Tutor at the Liverpool University Medical School, UK (e-mail: dcmt@liv.ac.uk).

Cees P M van der Vleuten is Professor in the Department of Educational Development and Research at the University of Maastricht, The Netherlands (e-mail: C.vanderVleuten@educ.unimaas.nl).

Laurence J Walsh is Professor in the School of Dentistry, University of Queensland, Brisbane, QLD, Australia (e-mail: l.walsh@mailbox.uq.edu.au).

Graham Webb is Professor and Director at the Centre for Higher Education Quality at Monash University, Melbourne, VIC, Australia (e-mail: Graham.Webb@adm.monash.edu.au).

Ineke H A P Wolfhagen is Associate Professor in the Department of Educational Development and Research at the University of Maastricht, The Netherlands (e-mail: I.Wolfhagen@educ.unimaas.nl).

Donald R Woods is Professor in the Chemical Engineering Department, McMaster University, Hamilton, ON, Canada (e-mail: woodsdr@mcmaster.ca).

INTRODUCTION

As soon as I heard about PBL..., it grabbed me! PBL sounded exciting, different and fun and I could see its relevance to the clinical situation in which my students' learning had to be applied. (Lovie-Kitchin, this volume)

I don't understand this problem-based curriculum, but I know it won't work. (Unidentified department chairman quoted by Abrahamson, 1997)

Problem-based learning (PBL) has stimulated and challenged teachers, learners and administrators worldwide to reflect on their educational philosophy and methods. Perhaps, like the case reporter from this book who wrote the first of the quotations above, you too have been intrigued by PBL and have thought about introducing it into your school or your own teaching. Perhaps you have been dissuaded from taking your intentions any further because of some of the concerns you and your colleagues have about what seems like a radical departure from traditional teaching/learning methods.

On the other hand, perhaps you are like the academic in the second quotation and either do not know what PBL is or do not yet understand it. (We hope, however, that you are *not* like him in having already made up your mind that it won't work!) This book will be of value to both sorts of people – and also to those who have already implemented PBL and want to learn more about it. This collection of case studies is unique in providing personal accounts of faculty as they contend with many of the common dilemmas faced by teachers and administrators who plan for and implement PBL. By learning from the compelling accounts of their experiences you can develop helpful strategies for when you use (or suggest using) PBL in your own curriculum.

INTRODUCTION TO PBL

Problem-based learning is a method of learning in which the learners first encounter a problem, followed by a systematic, student-centred enquiry process (Barrows and Tamblyn, 1980). Although the purpose of using problems in PBL is to stimulate learning of information and concepts brought out by the problems (rather than to 'solve' the problems), PBL does teach both a method of approaching and an attitude towards problem solving.

Typically in PBL, students work in small groups with a faculty tutor who acts as facilitator of discussions and of learning rather than as a direct source of information. During their work with a problem, students:

1. first encounter a problem 'cold', without doing any preparatory study in the area of the problem;
2. interact with each other to explore their existing knowledge as it relates to the problem;
3. form and test hypotheses about the underlying mechanisms that might account for the problem (up to their current levels of knowledge);
4. identify further learning needs for making progress with the problem;
5. undertake self-study between group meetings to satisfy the identified learning needs;
6. return to the group to integrate the newly gained knowledge and apply it to the problem;
7. repeat steps 3 to 6 as necessary; and
8. reflect on the process and on the content that has been learnt.

PBL in this form was first introduced at McMaster University Medical School in Canada in the late 1960s as its major teaching/learning approach. Several other medical schools (most notably Newcastle in Australia, Maastricht and New Mexico) followed during the 1970s. Since then, increasing numbers of schools and curricula, particularly but not solely in the professions, have implemented PBL. PBL has been used in virtually all of the health sciences, in social work, engineering, architecture, business, law, economics, management, mathematics, education, introductory university science, agriculture and other disciplines. PBL courses in secondary school have been reported. And examples of PBL curricula or courses can now be found in almost all parts of the world, including at least North and South America, Europe, Africa, the Middle East, Asia, Australia and the South Pacific.

By 1989, eight of the 127 medical schools in the United States had either totally PBL curricula or separate PBL tracks, while 96 others claimed to have 'some' PBL (Jonas et al, 1989). The claims by such a high proportion of US medical schools to use PBL reflect an evolution in the meaning of the term PBL. Howard Barrows, one of the originators of PBL, has on occasion implied that, to be called PBL, a programme must fit the description offered above (Barrows, 1985: 21–2). However, by 1986 he had also proposed a 'taxonomy of problem-based learning methods' and said that PBL 'does not refer to a specific educational method. It can have many different meanings'

(Barrows, 1986). Since then, others have described various spectra embracing educational approaches that might be termed PBL (Charlin *et al*, 1998; Harden and Davis, 1998).

For the purposes of this book of case studies, we have chosen to adopt a broad definition of the term, partly because it will be most widely applicable but also partly because even the less 'pure' forms of PBL are likely to confer many of the benefits of true PBL. Barrows (1986) has suggested that the main benefits are the structuring of knowledge for use in clinical contexts, the development of an effective clinical reasoning process, the development of effective self-directed learning skills and increased satisfaction with and motivation for learning. To these can be added the development of interpersonal, teamwork and communication skills, as well as the employment of small-group teaching methods, which are routinely applauded by students even in non-PBL contexts.

RESEARCH ON PBL

The increasing popularity of PBL in its many forms has been accompanied by increased interest among educational researchers in studying the effects of PBL. Notwithstanding the arguments about what teaching approaches qualify as PBL, many studies have looked at PBL from a number of perspectives, most frequently to investigate one or more of the following issues:

- the performance on assessments by students who have learnt using PBL, in comparison with those who have learnt by more traditional methods;
- the study behaviours and thought processes that are promoted by PBL;
- the satisfaction of students with PBL curricula;
- the adequacy of preparation of graduates by PBL curricula; and
- the satisfaction of faculty members with PBL curricula.

Unsurprisingly, given the relatively short history of PBL and the diversity of techniques that have been called PBL in the research literature, there are few definite conclusions about these issues. Researchers who have analysed the best designed studies since the inception of PBL (Albanese and Mitchell, 1993; Schmidt *et al*, 1987; Vernon and Blake, 1993) interpret the evidence as suggesting the following:

- Students from PBL curricula perform as well as or slightly less well than students from traditional curricula on conventional measures of their knowledge of basic medical sciences (although there is a good deal of heterogeneity in the findings due to curriculum-specific variations).
- Students from PBL curricula are superior to their counterparts from

traditional curricula with respect to their:
- approach to study (being more likely to study for understanding rather than for short-term recall);
- long-term retention of knowledge;
- clinical performance;
- knowledge of the clinical sciences;
- ratings by supervisors as postgraduates;
- motivation for learning;
- perceptions of their education (being more positive);
- perceptions of stress during their education (perceiving less stress); and
- use of resources for learning.
- Faculty members are more positive about their roles and about the students in PBL curricula than in traditional ones.
- The cost of running PBL curricula is comparable with that of running traditional ones for class sizes up to about 100.

Research on PBL is continuing, but it appears that being in PBL programmes certainly does not disadvantage students and may well confer a number of advantages. In addition, educational psychologists have shown that PBL conforms to sound educational principles (Norman and Schmidt, 1992; Regehr and Norman, 1996).

ISSUES IN PBL

Supporters of PBL claim that it is effective, relevant, exciting and fun. At the same time, it is also very different from traditional teaching methods and requires that administrators, teachers and students adapt. It demands of all three new knowledge, skills and behaviours, and it benefits from changed attitudes as well. As might be anticipated, proposals to introduce PBL elicit the resistance that can be faced by *any* sort of change (Bloom, 1989; Bouhuijs, 1990; Rogers, 1995), but there is also the more formidable resistance that is accorded to the sorts of large-scale, fundamental change represented by PBL (Bouhuijs, 1990; Mennin and Kaufman, 1989; Schwartz *et al*, 1994; Thompson and Williams, 1985).

Fortunately, there is research and development literature to assist in the process of change. There are also many books and manuals that can provide help to those wishing to develop PBL programmes, some of these resources even supplying examples (see the list of further reading at the end of this volume for a selection). As we shall soon explain, this book takes a different approach by having teachers describe their actual experiences of coping with some of the major issues arising during implementation of PBL. Although such issues are alluded to in most resources on PBL, they assume a stark reality in the stories recorded in this book because they represent important real dilemmas faced by the authors during their use of PBL. They include issues such as:

- the crucial role of administrative leadership and of sound governance in introducing PBL successfully;
- the need for 'buy in' and ownership of a PBL curriculum by faculty and staff;
- the importance of effective faculty development programmes in preparing staff for PBL;
- the value of effective communication and collaboration in preparing for the integrated approach utilized in PBL;
- the recognition of the need for students to take responsibility for their own learning during PBL and for teachers to facilitate that learning;
- the anxiety and concerns experienced by faculty as they recognize that they will have to turn over some control of the learning environment to students in PBL; and
- the necessity for assessment methods to be consistent with how students are learning in PBL.

INTRODUCTION TO THIS BOOK

While these are recurrent general issues in implementing PBL, it is probably the more immediate, practical concerns that discourage faculty who would like to try PBL from taking their intentions further – concerns such as the following:

- How can we overcome the political obstacles to the introduction of PBL?
- How can we convince teaching staff and students to accept PBL?
- How do we go about training teaching staff and students in the philosophy and methods of PBL?
- What issues do we have to consider in developing a suitable course structure for PBL?
- Won't students in a PBL course be in danger of leaving classes with misinformation?
- How can we go about assessing student performance in a PBL course?
- How do we deal with unproductive or dysfunctional groups in a PBL setting?
- How do we deal with individual problem students in PBL?
- What are some possible concerns if we want to continue PBL into the clinical part of a professional course?
- What issues do we have to consider if we want to adapt PBL to a

programme outside the health sciences?

All of these are important questions that are explored in this book through a series of case studies. The case studies are written by faculty members/ teachers who have actually grappled with these questions, developed their own responses to them, experienced the outcomes of those responses (for better or worse) and reflected on the lessons learnt.

The main aim of this book is to help people learn from the experience of the faculty members. The cases are structured in a way that is designed to place you, the reader, in realistic situations that other teachers have actually confronted. You will be asked to think about how you might have reacted to the situation if you had been in the case reporter's place, to assess how well the situation was actually handled, to consider what alternative responses were possible and to reflect on the implications the case has for your own circumstances.

The book considers many of the most important issues perceived and experienced by people who have tried PBL. You are invited to learn from their stories and, by reflecting on what you read, to prepare yourself to deal with similar issues and new challenges in PBL.

The book consists of 22 case studies that raise issues in three areas:

1. political/administrative/resource issues;
2. issues related to teachers, including their acceptance of the method, definition of their roles in PBL and teacher training for PBL; and
3. issues related to students, including their acceptance of PBL, classroom activities/dynamics/difficulties and assessment of student performance.

The cases are written by 37 faculty members from six different countries and from a range of disciplines and backgrounds, including medicine, dentistry, biomedical and natural sciences, architecture, engineering and optometry. The case writers all have at least one characteristic in common: they have first-hand experience of some of the important challenges that can arise during the implementation of PBL. While in many instances the actual participants in the stories have been disguised or the events dramatized somewhat, each case is based closely on an actual situation and its resolution. Contributors to the book were invited to tell stories of events and situations that they considered important and memorable.

Each case is preceded by an indication of the main issue or issues raised, and by some brief background information to set the context for the 'action'. The case proper consists of two or more parts, each concluding with a few questions for you to consider. We have introduced this reflective break between parts of a case at a point where an action must be taken and/or a decision made. You are invited to step into the writer's shoes at this point and decide not only what you think *should* be done next but also what you think *will actually happen* next given the circumstances of the case. After discovering what actually *did* happen, you will be asked to reflect on how the situation was handled and to consider some of the questions and issues raised by the case. At the end there is a case reporter's discussion that raises questions such as:

- How well was the situation handled?
- What other options might there have been for dealing with it?
- What lessons did the reporter and his or her colleagues learn from the experience?
- What lessons are there for others from the case?

The discussions are by no means exhaustive in that other important issues and/or questions could be examined, and you may well identify issues or perspectives that have not been mentioned. We sought to strike a balance between leaving each situation equivocal and open to individual interpretation on the one hand and tightly defining issues and providing guidance on the other. Nor is the discussion intended to give the 'right answer' to a problem. We do not believe that there is a simple and unequivocal 'right answer' in cases such as these, although, under the circumstances described, some solutions may be better than others. The purpose of the discussion is to explore the issues raised and to encourage you to make your own decisions based upon your interpretation of and reflections on the case. The intent is that you may then apply the insights gained from this experience as you deal with similar situations in your own implementation of PBL.

The book concludes with a brief list of suggested reading on problem-based learning and related issues. Most of the readings are of general applicability rather than being directed toward specific issues or events discussed in the cases. Again, the reading list is intended to be broad and immediately useful, rather than comprehensive. The editors and contributors would welcome enquiries from readers who would like more information. E-mail addresses are given for the editors and for at least one reporter for each case.

HOW TO USE THIS BOOK

We recommend that, as you read a case, you 'play the game' and read only Part 1, before reflecting and noting your impressions of what is going on, what courses of action could be taken next, what you think *will* happen next and what course of action *you* would pursue. The same applies to Part 2 (and further parts, where relevant). Questions have been provided at the end of each part of a case to assist you in framing your interpretation of and response to what is happening. In many instances, the questions are specific to the case, but some general questions that would be appropriate for most cases include the following.

At the end of Part 1, ask:

- What is going on here?
- What factors may have contributed to the situation described?
- How does the case reporter appear to see the situation?
- What *other* interpretations might there be?
- How might the situation be handled?
- What sorts of consequences might be expected from the possible actions?
- Given the nature of the participants, how will the situation probably be dealt with?

After the final part and the discussion, ask:

- How well was the situation handled?
- What general issues are brought out by the case?
- What do the case and its issues mean for me?

We believe that as an individual reader you will derive valuable insights if you use the case studies and discussions in this way. However, we suggest that you will also find it valuable to meet with colleagues to share impressions of the cases and insights obtained from them. The cases can serve as resources for advanced training and development of teaching staff and administrators. In fact, the cases presented in a previous book (Schwartz and Webb, 1993) were both the products of and the discussion materials for a series of group discussions in a faculty development programme. Others have also described the use of case studies in faculty development for teachers (Christensen, 1987; Hutchings, 1993; Wilkerson and Boehrer, 1992).

Whether done formally or informally, consideration of the cases and issues by groups of colleagues has benefits beyond those that may be obtained from individual reading. In discussions with colleagues, teachers can confront their own perceptions and readings of cases and face the possibility that others may not share their interpretations. Justifying these interpretations can bring teachers face-to-face with their philosophies of human nature and the nature of education. This can serve to stimulate them to become more reflective about their own practices. They may be challenged to come to terms with alternative conceptions and interpretations of each case. Teachers may be stimulated to re-examine and re-evaluate some of the central features of their own views by seeking to understand one another's interpretations and experiences and the outlooks that shape them. The discussion sections in this book may provide a starting point, but there are further opportunities for quality discussion between colleagues on these issues.

Reflection in teaching is crucial regardless of whether you read the cases as an individual or discuss them with colleagues. It is from this reflection that teachers are likely to obtain the most benefit from the cases (Fincher *et al*, 2000; Harden *et al*, 1999). Interestingly, the case *writers* themselves, in developing the cases for this book, discovered the value of reflecting on the educational experiences they reported. This is evidenced by the following comments they shared about the process:

> I have found [preparing my case] an interesting exercise and of course [it] led me to further reflection on my other teaching!

> I think both [of us] found that, the more we reflected on the incident, the more we could learn from and see in it. I guess this underlines how effective critical reflection can be in learning.

> Can I say that writing for the book was a very interesting experience to be part of – it did force me to think laterally and to reflect on some of the underlying things that I had mentally buried for some time. I guess revealing some of that is difficult!

We trust that your own reflection on the issues raised by the cases presented in this book will be just as valuable to you in making implementation of PBL at your school successful and rewarding.

References

Abrahamson, S (1997) 'Good planning is not enough', in ed D Boud and G I Feletti, *The Challenge of Problem-Based Learning*, 2nd edn, pp 53–57, Kogan Page, London

Albanese, M A and Mitchell, S (1993) 'Problem-based learning: a review of literature on its outcomes and implementation issue', *Academic Medicine*, **68**, pp 52–81

Barrows, H S (1985) *How to Design a Problem-Based Curriculum for the Preclinical Years*, Springer, New York

Barrows, H S (1986) 'A taxonomy of problem-based learning methods', *Medical Education*, **20**, pp 481–86

Barrows, H S and Tamblyn, R N (1980) *Problem-Based Learning: An approach to medical education*, Springer, New York

Bloom, S W (1989) 'The medical school as a social organization: the sources of resistance to change', *Medical Education*, **23**, pp 228–41

Bouhuijs, P A J (1990) 'The maintenance of educational innovations in medical schools', in ed Z M Nooman, H G Schmidt and E S Ezzat, *Innovation in Medical Education: An evaluation of its present status*, pp 175–88, Springer, New York

Charlin, B, Mann, K and Hansen, P (1998) 'The many faces of problem-based learning: a framework for understanding and comparison', *Medical Teacher*, **20**, pp 323–30

Christensen, C R (1987) *Teaching and the Case Method*, Harvard Business School, Boston, MA

Fincher, R-M E, Simpson, D E, Mennin, S P, Rosenfeld, G C, Rothman, A, Cole McGrew, M, Hansen, P A, Mazmanian, P E and Turnbull, J M (2000) 'Scholarship in teaching: an imperative for the 21st century', *Academic Medicine*, **75**, pp 887–94

Harden, R M and Davis, M H (1998) 'The continuum of problem-based learning', *Medical Teacher*, **20**, pp 317–22

Harden, R M, Grant, J, Buckley, G and Hart, I R (1999) 'BEME Guide No. 1: best evidence medical education', *Medical Teacher*, **21**, pp 553–62

Hutchings, P (1993) *Using Cases to Improve College Teaching: A guide to more reflective practice*, American Association for Higher Education, Washington, DC

Jonas, H S, Etzel, S I and Barzansky, B (1989) 'Undergraduate medical education', *Journal of the American Medical Association*, **262**, pp 1011–19

Mennin, S P and Kaufman, A (1989) 'The change process and medical education', *Medical Teacher*, **11**, pp 9–16

Norman, G R and Schmidt, H G (1992) 'The psychological basis of problem-based learning: a review of the evidence', *Academic Medicine*, **67**, pp 557–65

Regehr, G and Norman, G R (1996) 'Issues in cognitive psychology: implications for professional education', *Academic Medicine*, **71**, pp 988–1001

Rogers, E M (1995) *Diffusion of Innovations*, The Free Press, New York

Schmidt, H G, Dauphinee, W D and Patel, V L (1987) 'Comparing the effects of problem-based and conventional curricula in an international sample', *Journal of Medical Education*, **62**, pp 305–15

Schwartz, P L, Heath, C J and Egan, A G (1994) *The Art of the Possible. Ideas from a traditional medical school engaged in curricular revision*, University of Otago Press, Dunedin, New Zealand

Schwartz, P and Webb, G (1993) *Case Studies on Teaching in Higher Education*, Kogan Page, London

Thompson, D G and Williams, R G (1985) 'Barriers to the acceptance of problem-based learning in medical schools', *Studies in Higher Education*, **10**, pp 199–204

Vernon, D T A and Blake, R L (1993) 'Does problem-based learning work? A meta-analysis of evaluative research', *Academic Medicine*, **68**, pp 550–63

Wilkerson, L and Boehrer, J (1992) 'Using cases about teaching for faculty development', *To Improve the Academy*, **11**, pp 253–62

SECTION 1

POLITICAL, ADMINISTRATIVE AND RESOURCE ISSUES

CHAPTER 1

COME AND SEE THE REAL THING

Case reporters: David Prideaux, Bren Gannon, Elizabeth Farmer, Sue Runciman and Isobel Rolfe

Issues raised

This case study focuses on some of the methods that can be used to try to convince faculty members to accept a proposal to adopt PBL within a medical curriculum.

Background

The School of Medicine at Flinders University in Adelaide is, by Australian standards, relatively small and recent. The first class was admitted in 1974. The current intake comprises 58 domestic students and a further 25 full fee paying overseas students. In 1996, the School was the first in Australia to move from the traditional six-year, undergraduate-entry medical course to a four-year, graduate-entry course.

PART 1

The Faculty at Flinders decided in 1991 to move to a four-year, graduate-entry medical course. At the time, a small but enthusiastic group of staff, including some who had worked in similar programmes in other medical schools, advocated the adoption of PBL as the main teaching/learning method for the new course. Similar proposals had been considered but rejected in the 1974 six-year curriculum and its subsequent revisions. During 1992, four staff members attended a five-day Medical Curriculum Workshop at Harvard University and they returned to become key advocates for PBL. One of the four subsequently travelled extensively at his own expense to gain information on and experience in PBL in medical education. The end result was that the PBL Working Party was one of the first groups to be established in the decision-making structures for the new programme. One of its main tasks was to convince the majority of the staff in the School to embrace the PBL approach.

There was a history of curriculum reform in the School, with three major revisions of the six-year course having been undertaken prior to the decision to adopt graduate entry. A high level of collegial decision making had characterized earlier curricular establishment and revision. A fundamental component of that process was the Annual Curriculum Conference, during which staff moved off campus for a day and a half to discuss significant educational issues. An additional Curriculum Conference had been called in 1991 to consider and decide upon the adoption of a graduate-entry course.

The Conference Organizing Committee and the PBL Working Party developed a plan to devote the 1993 Curriculum Conference to an introduction to PBL for School of Medicine staff. We hoped that this would lead to a decision by the whole School to adopt the approach in the new course. We knew that there would be other opportunities to promote our message, but the Curriculum Conference was the big chance. The stakes were high. What could we do at the Conference that would have the best chance of convincing faculty members to accept PBL?

If you had the task of organizing the Faculty Conference and wanted to promote PBL, what would you do?
What do you think was actually done?

PART 2

For better or worse, we decided to adapt the old adage: 'experience is the best teacher' and we developed a three-part plan. The first two parts consisted of two staff participation exercises that we organized for the Conference. The first, on the tutorial process, was brought back from the University of New Mexico by the key staff member who had studied PBL extensively at other institutions and who was now co-chair of the PBL Working Party. The second was used with the kind permission of the Faculty of Architecture at the University of Newcastle and centred on a PBL exercise involving the design of a bird hide (a concealed place for watching birds). We deliberately chose a non-medical 'case' because we feared that some clinical staff might move quickly to a rapid diagnosis with a medical case and not engage fully in the processes of PBL.

The third part of our plan for the Curriculum Conference was to provide a live demonstration of PBL. The newly appointed Dean of the School of Medicine had come from Newcastle University which, at the time, was the only Australian medical school to use PBL. He offered to use his contacts to bring a group of students and their tutor from Newcastle to participate in a tutorial in front of the Flinders staff. Significantly, he also undertook to fund the transport and accommodation costs for this demonstration. Those of us who were planning the Curriculum Conference placed two conditions on the exercise. First, the tutorial group was to be a regular one engaged in its normal case of the week. Second, the tutor was to be the group's regular one, albeit one of the acknowledged 'better' tutors at Newcastle. A tutor was subsequently invited to make the trip with her normal group.

The Conference was set for a day and a half in October 1993. There was a large attendance, in excess of the 100–120 who usually attended such events, and expectations were high. The first morning began with the two staff participation exercises. If the aim of these exercises was to achieve staff consensus in support of introducing PBL, then we had a feeling that they had not fared well. This was especially true for the 'bird hide' exercise. Staff were allocated to groups to respond to a scenario that asked them to design a bird hide for the university lake using recycled materials. The exercise encouraged some frivolity, lightheartedness and competition between the various staff tutorial groups. Underneath this veneer of conviviality, however, the exercise exposed some substantive concerns about PBL. These were raised in plenary feedback sessions at the end of the small group activity. There were four major issues:

1. PBL appeared to be 'time wasting and inefficient'. Basic points were subject to prolonged discussion rather than being resolved quickly. It was questioned whether Flinders could afford the luxury of extended time being spent in discussion, given that the course was being reduced from six to four years.
2. There was a strong view that the exercise had resulted in the pooling of 'collective ignorance'. Who was going to provide the correct explanations and how would these be recognized as correct?
3. Allied to the point above was an expressed concern about the lack of an 'expert' tutor. In the absence of such a person, who would rule on 'incorrect' or 'irrelevant' ideas?
4. The final issue concerned assessment. It was claimed that PBL would be constrained by assessment and the need to prepare for examinations. We had unwittingly brought this issue to the fore because we had added, for fun, an assessment of the bird hide design by a selected panel consisting of the Newcastle students and their tutor. This drove much of the staff group work. In light of what we all now know about how assessment drives learning, we should, perhaps, have avoided introducing this part of the exercise.

By lunchtime, some of us judged that, had a motion to adopt PBL been put at that time, it would have gone down. A couple of us chose to take our lunch outside in the October sun for some relief from what we saw as impending doom. Perhaps we would have been better off engaging in some reflection on what we could (and perhaps should) have done to manage the morning sessions better. We should have asked ourselves some of the following questions:

- What was the effect of the decision to use the bird hide example? Did it trivialize the exercise? Would a medical example have been better?
- How well were we prepared to handle important and predictable questions of 'time wasting', 'collective ignorance' and 'expert tutors'? These were common issues in the literature. Had we thought through how they might be handled?
- Why did we put the assessment exercise in? What purpose was it supposed to serve? Again, did this act to trivialize the whole exercise?

After lunch, the demonstration of PBL began. The tutor and eight Newcastle students sat in a 'fishbowl' at the front of a tiered lecture theatre with 100 or so Flinders staff looking on. The students were wired up so that all could hear their voices and they were under the glare of strong lighting. One roving and one fixed studio TV camera recorded the demonstration on video for posterity. This was hardly the stuff of a routine tutorial!

Conference planning committee members took their seats in the front row of the lecture theatre. Given the way the morning's session had unfolded, some of us were slumped low in our seats. We continued to sink lower as the demonstration began and audio-visual staff tried to sort out technical problems with the sound and recording system that had caused the students to be inaudible to the gathered staff observers. We wondered, 'Could the Conference reach any lower point than this?'

The case under discussion began with a video vignette of a female patient with abdominal pain. It began slowly as sound problems were corrected and the students got used to the glaring lights. But the momentum picked up as the students went through the classic steps of PBL and soon they seemed to forget or ignore their unfamiliar surroundings and the presence of their audience. The problem was discussed, key information lists generated, hypotheses constructed, further information was sought, learning issues were identified, learning goals were set and group processes were observed. Most importantly, in all of this the tutor said very little. We began to sit up straighter in our seats. Was the tide beginning to turn?

What came next sealed the fate of PBL at Flinders. At the conclusion of the PBL tutorial, a decision was made to cancel an 'expert panel' session that was to provide a commentary on the exercise in favour of an 'all in' plenary where the students and tutor were challenged by questions from the Flinders staff and responded accordingly. The students provided answers to many of the issues raised by Flinders staff earlier in the day. The charge of time wasting in PBL was dealt with quickly. One of the students responded: 'The question is, how much more time would I waste if I went away and tried to learn all this on my own?'

Similarly, they outlined mechanisms for dealing with 'incorrect' information and discussed the role of the tutor in guiding and facilitating learning. The students were able to demonstrate that they were well advanced in the process of making the tutor redundant as they moved to the end of their block of time with her. The climax came towards the end of question time. One of the senior Flinders staff members asked the students to indicate who had come straight from high school and who had other experiences before beginning the five-year undergraduate course at Newcastle. The challenge was thrown back to the staff member by one of the students: 'Would you like to try to identify which of us entered straight from high school?' No one in the audience could or was willing to do it. The intent of the question had obviously been to establish whether the sophisticated thinking displayed by the group was a result of PBL or prior experience. The returned challenge provided most of the answer; the rest came when the challenging student, who had clearly been one of the most active students during the tutorial, revealed herself as being straight from high school.

The discussion continued both formally and informally throughout the Conference, but the Organizing Committee had a newfound confidence. What emerged was that the Flinders staff were particularly impressed with at least three things:

1. the high level of motivation displayed by the Newcastle students;
2. the high level of critical thinking and problem solving displayed; and
3. the impressive knowledge base demonstrated by the students.

The Newcastle students were judged to be far superior to our own students in the existing six-year course at Flinders on these attributes. PBL was on its way to being adopted at Flinders. No more slumping in seats!

Why did observation of students engaged in an actual PBL session have such a profound effect? Why did participation exercises for faculty fail to work? What other methods might be used to convince faculty to accept PBL? What are the implications of this case for other schools wishing to introduce PBL?

CASE REPORTERS' DISCUSSION

For us this case raises two major issues in curriculum change. The first is the importance of building upon existing patterns of decision making in planning the change. There was a need to move the advocacy of PBL from the small group of supporters to what Fullan (1992) and others have described as 'ownership' of the methodology by a much wider group of staff in the School. Clearly, the Curriculum Conference provided a well-tried option to do this, but there were risks. The Curriculum Conference could have offered the opportunity for power blocs opposing PBL to form. These can sometimes be quite influential in preventing significant change. The outcome of the Conference could have gone either way: support for or rejection of PBL as the main teaching methodology in the new course. Prior to the live tutorial demonstration it had appeared to be headed for the latter.

The second issue was the use of the live demonstration of PBL. We describe PBL as 'its own best advocate'. Up to that point, we had recommended readings about PBL, held discussions about PBL and even got staff participating in exercises that were contrived, designed or borrowed, but all of them were of little avail. In the end, there was no substitute for coming to see the 'real thing'. We would claim that the demonstration was the real thing, albeit with a degree of artificiality introduced by the cameras, lights and sound system, and by the audience of interested and critical onlookers. In the final analysis, however, the Newcastle students were a normal student group, with their regular, although specially selected tutor, and they were working with their prescribed case for the week. It was not a demonstration exercise. Thus the stakes were high for the students as well as for the Conference planning group. The students had to achieve their learning goals for the case while at the same time demonstrating the worth of the PBL process. This is in marked contrast to the 'bird hide' case undertaken by the staff. It was not a 'real' problem and was probably of little interest to most staff. Nor was there any pressure on them to learn something. In retrospect, we wonder whether the staff could ever have been expected to work in the same way as the students on such an exercise.

The discussion following the demonstration was every bit as important as the demonstration itself. It showed that the PBL students had sophisticated thinking skills, could reflect upon and articulate their learning processes and were not necessarily intimidated by an audience of academics of all levels of seniority. For example, they were quite happy to tell the tutor that they were working to make her 'redundant' in front of such an august group. However, what made the discussion particularly telling was that the students could refer to the substantive learning goals they generated and how they would be followed up. They could point out the actual processes they went through and the genuine issues they faced in working through the problem as a group. This was no artificial exercise.

It was also not a cheap exercise. The reality came at a price and not every institution wishing to adopt PBL may be able to afford such a grand scheme. Further, not all potential demonstrators of PBL may be prepared to disrupt their normal tutorial process and take their 'show' to the other end of the country and under the scrutiny of onlookers. Having a newly appointed dean who had come from Newcastle was a clear advantage. Nevertheless, what this case study shows is that authentic demonstrations of PBL in themselves may well be a better investment in staff development than readings, workshops and seminars. Other forms of demonstration that are not as expensive may need to be found. In the end, however, the costs of providing other forms of staff development in PBL must be balanced against the seemingly more expensive option of importing a group and tutor from elsewhere. It may well prove to be the less expensive option in the long run.

Reference

Fullan, M (1992) *Successful School Improvement: The implementation perspective and beyond*, Open University Press, Buckingham

CHAPTER 2

No MONEY WHERE YOUR MOUTH IS

Case reporter: Nina Felice Schor

Issues raised

This case raises the issue of the time- and people-intensiveness of PBL relative to more traditional approaches to teaching. When revenue-generating service obligations compete with teaching for time and faculty, teachers and their administrative leaders may be unwilling to contribute to teaching.

Background

The medical school course that forms the basis for this case was initiated in April of 1994 as part of a massive curricular revision. In the first year of the course, recruiting facilitators was relatively easy. Enthusiasm for the new curriculum was high, publicity was everywhere, and the economic and professional pressures that managed medical care would soon pose were not yet prominent. The events recounted in the case occurred in December of 1998, by which time the initial excitement associated with the new curriculum had dissipated and economic forces had conspired to make high-volume delivery of clinical service the number one priority of clinical departments in the medical school.

PART 1

Dr Aronson walked from his office into the secretarial area. 'Ms Hartman? Did those letters to the department chairs all go out?'

Ms Hartman briefly stopped typing into the computer and looked in his direction. 'Yes. They were all mailed last Tuesday.'

Dr Aronson shook his head in dismay. 'Each year this becomes more and more of a problem', he thought. Each year, since he began directing his PBL course for second-year students, it became harder and harder to get faculty facilitators. He would give it one more week and then he would send each Chair another letter marked as a 'second request'.

By the time a week had elapsed, the Chairs of Pharmacology and Neurobiology had each submitted names to him as their faculty participants in the course. That left Biochemistry, Physiology and all of the clinical departments. How was he ever going to get all of the facilitators trained and ready to go by April?

He drafted a second letter to each of the other Chairs and had Ms Hartman send these out. Two days later, Ms Hartman buzzed him on the intercom. 'Dr Lawrence is on the phone. He wants to talk to you about the course you give for the second-year students.' Dr Lawrence was the Chair of the Department of Surgery. If he took time out of his day to call, it must be really important.

'Hi, Sam', Dr Aronson said into the phone. 'What can I do for you?'

'Well, Mort, I got this request from you again for facilitators for your course. You know we've always sent you people in the past, and in fact they've all enjoyed their involvement. But with the course going from 9 to 11 each morning – well, our surgery schedule starts at 7.30. How can we allow someone to take two hours out of the surgery schedule for two or three mornings a week for four or five weeks? Do you know how much money the department would lose? Do you have any idea how backed up the elective surgery schedule would become? Maybe you could let whomever we give you from our department precept their particular groups between 5 and 7 am, so they're clear by the time the surgery schedule begins.'

'C'mon, Sam. You know that would never work. First of all, the computers are time-gated, so no one can access information from that repository before the time the course meets. It would be a fiasco to have one or two groups able to pass information on to their colleagues before some of the sessions take place. And besides, which of the students would come between 5 and 7 when the rest of the class is meeting between 9 and 11? Be realistic! We're not a group practice or a community hospital, Sam. We're an academic institution!'

Dr Lawrence laughed wistfully. 'Get real, Mort. You know as well as I that the hospital CEO is breathing down my neck to do twice as many cases with half as many staff. I'll do what I can. I always have. But I can't guarantee we can give you anyone. No one is willing to pay for teaching, and everyone has to generate his or her salary or we're all up the creek.'

Dr Aronson hung up and found himself longing for the good old days when teaching a medical school class meant finding one faculty member willing to teach each major topic. This assembling of a team, each of whom teaches only 9 or 10 students at a time, is an impossible dream.

Still, he wasn't prepared to give up. 'Ms Hartman, please get me Dr Gorlakis in Endocrinology', Dr Aronson said into the telephone. He hung up, and minutes later his intercom buzzed. 'Okay. Put him through.' The telephone rang.

'Ned, it's Mort. I need to ask you something. You taught in the case studies course last year. What do you think? Would you do it again? Is it worth your time and effort?'

'You know I enjoyed teaching the course. The students were great, the cases were fun, the computer kept me from worrying that I was forgetting to tell them something. But I'll be honest with you, Mort. McDuffy is on my case again. Says teaching doesn't bring money into the department. Tells me I need to see a new patient every 20 minutes and a revisit every 10. Three hours in the course is 15 patients not seen, not billed. I'm not sure I can do it without losing my job.'

Dr Aronson finally decided that he had to do something – he would talk with the Dean.

Two days later, as he sat in the Dean's Office waiting room, he wondered if he was making a mistake. After all, he was just an Assistant Professor. How would the Dean react to his concern about the increasing difficulty he was having getting faculty to teach? Maybe he should just keep his mouth shut. Too late! Here comes the Dean....

How should Dr Aronson approach this meeting with the Dean?
If you were the Dean, what would be your reaction to Dr Aronson?
How do you think the Dean actually will react?

PART 2

Dean Kalmus came out of his office and greeted him warmly. 'Mort, come on in. Sorry to keep you waiting. I hear your case studies course is rapidly becoming the jewel in the crown of the new curriculum! You know, I just spoke at an alumni luncheon about this switch to PBL. You could feel the excitement in the room. Maybe we should host tours of the PBL rooms for the alumni.'

'Actually, that's sort of why I'm here. You know, it's got harder and harder each year to get faculty to teach in the course. Everyone enjoys it, but all the Chairs take points off towards promotion if you teach instead of seeing patients. Half the departments are imposing a 10 per cent salary-at-risk policy, contingent on fulfilling a quota of outpatient visits. No one can afford to teach no matter how exciting the curriculum is.'

Dean Kalmus's grin never left his face. 'You know, what goes around comes around. We had problems like this all the time when I was in your shoes. But once the students make their excitement and appreciation clear at the next Curriculum Colloquium, why you'll have faculty begging to be part of your course. And of course you know no one's promotion will get past the

Promotions Committee without outstanding teaching credentials. Don't worry, Mort. Word'll get around.'

Dr Aronson couldn't believe how naive the Dean was. Pats on the back don't mean anything when your salary is cut for all your efforts. 'Somehow there needs to be a hedge against the negative incentives of the Chairs. Is there some way the Medical School could pay faculty members based on how much teaching they do?'

Dean Kalmus's grin got broader. 'You know Medical School revenues emanate from the Dean's tax levied on each department's practice plan. You know better than I how clinical revenues to the practice plans are declining with managed care. From where do you propose I take the money to reimburse our faculty for teaching? Payment for teaching is and always has been the joy of teaching itself.'

As he slowly made his way back to his room with a solution no closer, Dr Aronson found himself wondering from what planet the Dean had descended.

What do you think about the way this problem was handled by Dr Aronson? By the Dean?
What, if any, help could Dr Aronson have requested from the Dean?
What would you propose as a short-term solution and a long-term strategy to deal with this situation?

PART 3

Dr Aronson spent much of the weekend trying to decide whether to resign his directorship of the course or try a new and different approach to the recruitment of faculty. He had always loved teaching and had passed up more lucrative jobs to become a university professor. This course was the essence of who he was – a chance to make a difference for classes of students not just now but for years to come. There had to be a better way to make it tangibly worth the faculty facilitators' time and effort. By Monday morning he had a plan.

'Ms Hartman? Please get Sam Norita from the Faculty Affairs Office on the phone.' Yes. This was the way to do it. He had thought it through thoroughly and was convinced that somehow he had to get people to understand how valuable teaching was to the Medical School. If he couldn't get direct monies to put behind it, at least he could get career advancement.

His intercom buzzed. 'Hi, Sam. Hope I didn't catch you at a bad time. I wanted to get your input on an idea I had over the weekend. You know how all of us trying to recruit facilitators for our PBL-based courses have been having trouble because most of the Chairs put pressure on faculty to get grants and see patients?... Yeah... I got to thinking about this, and I wonder whether it might be worth talking to the Tenured Faculty Promotions [TFP] Committee about the weight they put on teaching as a component of the CVs of people coming up for promotion… Well, once they were on-board with this, we could get them to send a directive to each of the Chairs emphasizing the importance of teaching as part of the portfolio. My sense is that, once it's clear that teaching is necessary and, in extraordinary cases, sufficient for promotion, it will be a lot harder for Chairs to discourage junior faculty from taking on teaching assignments… Good. I'd be glad to speak at the next TFP Committee meeting. I'll have my secretary put it on my calendar… Thanks, Sam.'

The next week, Dr Aronson presented to the Tenured Faculty Promotions Committee the double-bind of, on the one hand, making teaching a critical component of the mission of the Medical School and, on the other hand, penalizing faculty of the Medical School for taking time out from research and clinical work to teach. He and Dr Norita, Chair of the Committee, emphasized the need for career advancement as a reward for mission-critical activities that do not bring in revenue. They then drafted a memo that was distributed to all of the Chairs of departments at the Medical School impressing upon them the critical need for teaching in the dossiers of those who are being put up for promotion. In addition, they stressed the conviction of the TFP Committee and its Chair that teaching of extraordinary quantity, quality and/or innovativeness should be regarded as decreasing the requirements for service and research components of the dossier. Much to Dr Aronson's delight, the TFP Committee followed with a 'promotion checklist' to be used as a guide for junior faculty members and their mentors and Chairs that included a place in which to account for number of classes taught, the nature of these classes, number of students per class and leadership or directorship roles in teaching and curriculum design. Most unbelievably, the Dean proposed to the Executive Committee of the Medical School a new formula for the allocation of funds to each department that included hours spent by department members in teaching activities.

The year in which this took place, Dr Aronson and his colleagues barely squeaked by with enough facilitators to teach their course. It took until the following year to see the fruits of the labours of the TFP Committee, Aronson and Norita. But what fruit it was! Many of the Chairs were suggesting the names of junior faculty members who needed teaching experience and credit. Faculty who had previously taught in the course and enjoyed it wanted to do it again now that it did not carry the financial 'stigma' to the departments and perhaps carried some credit towards promotion and tenure.

What other methods might be used to encourage faculty to participate as PBL tutors?

How can the monetary costs of teaching in a system like PBL be balanced against the intangible gains of the positive educational environment?

What might be the roles of leadership and governance in dealing with this situation?

CASE REPORTER'S DISCUSSION

The problem faced by Dr Aronson, and indeed by his medical school in general, is one that is dealt with on a daily basis in settings where the same individuals are responsible for both teaching and revenue generation. The desire to teach drove many faculty members in such institutions to take academic positions and forgo the higher salaries offered by practice in the private sector. None the less, the erosion of sources of money to finance time spent in teaching has forced these individuals to justify their existence by bringing in the whole of their salaries through research grants and non-academic service. Chairs of academic departments that have a service component have increasingly put pressure on these faculty members to limit their teaching commitments and increase the time they spend in revenue-generating activities.

To make matters more challenging, the move away from the lecture format and towards PBL and other small-group activities has increased the number of teacher-hours required per class. While more rewarding for both teacher and student, PBL requires a larger commitment – both temporal and personal – than more traditional teaching approaches do.

Many schools that include a service component have begun having faculty members and departments compile information about their individual and collective contributions to the teaching done at that institution. Such data are used to derive an 'Education Compensation Unit' (ECU) based score for each faculty member and/or department. Allocations of medical school monies to each department are generally prorated based on the number of ECUs accrued by its members. The chair of that department is expected, although not universally required, to in turn allocate salary 'incentive' monies to the department's faculty members who provided 'teaching service' to the medical school. In many institutions in the United States, some percentage of each non-tenured faculty member's salary is placed 'at risk', and restitution of that fraction of the salary is contingent on the fiscal status of the whole department. The acquisition of ECUs by a department then becomes one way to work towards salary restitution for all of its faculty members. As was the case for Dr Aronson, so too have course directors at the University of Pittsburgh School of Medicine had an easier time recruiting faculty facilitators (especially from the ranks of junior faculty) since departmental support and individual promotion have been more tightly linked to teaching contributions.

One of the most difficult issues for schools embarking upon a PBL-rich curriculum is the cultivation of the kind of leadership and culture needed to support such curricula. The case presented illustrates the difficulties that arise when a new curriculum is adopted in the setting of an 'old' governance and leadership paradigm. The dean was used to having things happen because he willed them to; the course director was used to having his direction, guidance and reward come from the dean; the faculty were used to teaching in the traditional way in which they were taught and being compensated in the traditional monetary way in which their teachers were compensated. New curricula require a new infrastructure, and the impetus for development and adoption of such an infrastructure may have to come from the bottom up rather than from the top down. At the University of Pittsburgh, just as in Dean Kalmus's medical school, it was the cry of the students and junior faculty, as heard and acted upon by the Tenured Faculty Promotions and Appointments Committee and the Office for Medical Education, that 'taught' the Dean and Chairs what to do. The Medical School experience has in turn become the impetus for the initiation of university-wide teaching excellence seminars, PBL workshops and sessions for faculty and administrative leaders on financing and rewarding teaching.

Although incompletely answered in the case, there are fundamental questions that should be considered by any faculty that is in a position similar to ours. The answers may be different at each medical school, but without answers the issues raised by the questions may well jeopardize the long-term success of labour-intensive teaching methods like PBL:

- Who should be paying for the increased faculty requirement constituted by PBL curricula?
- What safeguards can an institution put in place for those faculty who are successful at teaching but who do not generate their salaries doing so?
- Can the faculty-intensive nature of PBL be altered without undoing its very fabric?
- Is there merit to the idea of hiring a separate contingent of faculty members primarily to teach (as distinct from those of whom non-academic service is expected)?
- Are the benefits of PBL to teacher, student and institution sufficient to justify its high cost?

CHAPTER 3

Into the Lion's Den

Case reporter: Amy Blue

Issues raised

This case study looks at problems arising when PBL is introduced into a new, combined third-year medicine and surgery teaching attachment (clerkship).

Background

The events described took place at a mid-sized medical school in south-eastern USA. At the time of these events (1993) the school was undergoing significant change throughout all four years of its curriculum. Major changes included the introduction of problem-based learning and the development of interdisciplinary courses, including interdisciplinary clerkships in the traditionally discipline-specific third year.

PART 1

I clearly remember the interview for my first medical education position, that of curriculum consultant in the school's newly developed Medical Education Office. The Associate Dean for Academic Affairs told me, 'The implementation of the new third-year combined medicine-surgery clerkship isn't going well.' One of my principal responsibilities would be to replace an existing curriculum consultant who had been assigned to facilitate development of this new clerkship. I was told that Dr Kammer, the clerkship director for Surgery, and Dr Ciproni, the clerkship director for Medicine, were dedicated teachers and were enthusiastic about the new clerkship, but 'differences in opinion' between them about the development of the clerkship had undermined its implementation. During my interview, the Associate Dean warned: 'Dr Kammer has a strong personality', without further elaboration. I wondered how this 'strong personality' would manifest itself.

The day I started the job, I learnt that the clerkship's first rotation of students had become very disenchanted with its organization and implementation. Many of the 36 students had signed a student-initiated petition asking the Dean to separate the combined clerkship back to two traditional clerkships. 'Disorganized activities with faculty unprepared for them and no apparent educational benefit to a combined clerkship' characterized their complaints. A meeting to discuss the students' concerns was scheduled with the Dean, the chairmen of the Internal Medicine and Surgery Departments, the Associate Dean for Academic Affairs, Drs Kammer and Ciproni, myself and an Internal Medicine Fellow, Dr Grey, who was assisting Dr Ciproni with the educational aspects of the Internal Medicine portion of the clerkship.

During this meeting, Dr Kammer made disparaging remarks regarding the Medical Education Office staff's lack of knowledge about medical education. Though not directly named, I took this comment as a personal insult – it was my introduction to his 'strong personality'! Shortly after the meeting, I told Dr Kammer, 'I'm not the same as my predecessor (the previous curriculum consultant) – I've been trained in PBL here at the school and used it while teaching third-year medical students last year'. My goal with this confrontation was to establish the legitimacy of my professional qualifications with him. He acknowledged the ineptness of my predecessor and said nothing further.

The result of the meeting with the Deans and chairmen was that the clerkship would continue as planned and the Dean told the two departments to 'work out your differences'. I saw my first role to be a detective to uncover what had led to the current crisis. My predecessor, who was still in the office but assigned other duties, blamed most of the trouble on Dr Kammer and his personality. As a newcomer, I didn't want to confront her with the information that others attributed the clerkship's problems to her lack of organizational ability. My stance with her was to agree: 'Everyone involved is difficult', which most days was a sincere thought.

If I were to believe faculty and staff associated with the clerkship, all difficulties were the other party's fault – the surgeons were dictatorial, demanding and inflexible, while the internists were disorganized, had no experience with educational innovation and had 'no backbone'. These depictions had elements of truth to them. My primary thought was not to form an alliance with either departmental side, but to remain a neutral party. My role was to facilitate negotiation and productive activity so that a well-administered educational experience for faculty and students would result. The concept of the combined clerkship was not a source of dispute. What was clear from my conversations with faculty, other staff and clerkship students was that the main difficulty was the disorganization and poor planning of the clerkship's problem-based learning programme. Specific problems included:

- Several case topics were peripheral and of questionable importance for third-year students: restrictive cardiomyopathy secondary to amyloidosis, acoustic neuroma as a presentation for multiple endocrine neoplasia syndrome, and septic shock as tuberculosis.
- Many cases were not written clearly, their presentation was difficult for faculty and students to follow, and students were unsure if they were getting important factual information from the experience.
- Case materials were distributed to faculty at the last minute, giving them insufficient time to review the case (or know where it was in their office).
- The timing of the PBL sessions (6.30–8.00 am) and their frequency (three times a week) 'interfered' with students' clinical responsibilities, particularly when students were on the Medicine part of their clerkship.

This looked like more than enough difficulties for one clerkship! Clearly, something had to be done. But what?

What might be some of the factors underlying this problem?
If you were faced with these problems in a course, what strategies and tactics would you use to solve them?
What would your priorities be?

PART 2

I decided that the most effective solutions would be those that Drs Kammer, Ciproni and Grey developed themselves, and my responsibility would be to provide the support to implement those solutions. To start with, soon after the meeting with the Deans and chairmen, Dr Kammer unilaterally assumed the leadership role for the clerkship and began to negotiate more curricular clerkship decisions with the Internal Medicine Fellow, Dr Grey, rather than with Dr Ciproni. It was understood that Dr Grey would become the Internal Medicine Clerkship director in the next academic year. These negotiations went smoothly, though the interactions placed Dr Grey in an unenviable position vis-à-vis Dr Ciproni, his superior. The presence of Dr Grey certainly made my life easier. The suggestions put forward by Dr Kammer, which were educationally very sound, were negotiated easily and not rejected outright, as was often the case with Dr Ciproni. This helped me focus on the organizational details of the clerkship, which were my responsibility.

We recognized that the PBL curriculum needed a major reorganization. First came the task of deciding the clinical topics on which the PBL cases would be based. Drs Kammer, Ciproni and Grey, with feedback from other faculty, each developed a list of topics from their disciplines that they believed were essential for third-year students to learn about. Two considerations were paramount in developing these and the final list: 1) the institution's goal of producing generalist physicians, and 2) the patient conditions routinely encountered or not encountered by students during their ward rotations. Given the 16-week length of the clerkship, with one week for orientation and one for examinations, it was agreed to develop a core of 14 cases, each focused on a single disease process, with secondary conditions and psychosocial topics woven into the cases.

Examples of primary topics included myocardial infarction, lung cancer, trauma and shock, claudication, and human immunodeficiency virus (HIV). The secondary topics were medical and surgical conditions routinely encountered in inpatient settings (such as hypertension and wound infections); psychosocial issues included patient compliance, ethics, etc. Dr Kammer readily acknowledged that many of the cases were more 'medical' in nature, but they would none the less provide the students with pertinent clinical information for surgery.

The next challenge was to facilitate the PBL case-writing process for designated authors. This involved three primary tasks: author assignment, provision of a case description to authors, and timeline vigilance. A primary author was designated for each case, based on the person's expertise in a particular clinical field. Suggested co-authors were colleagues from the other discipline who we knew could work effectively with the primary authors to provide appropriate additional information. Case authors were given a paragraph outlining the essentials we wanted in the case: patient presentation of problem, important physical or laboratory findings, diagnosis, treatment and patient outcome. In addition, case objectives were included to further guide the author's development of the case. Finally, we set a timeline for production of first and second drafts, and one of my jobs was to provide the 'friendly reminder' of when the case needed to be complete. Drs Kammer and Grey, myself and other faculty reviewed and edited first and second drafts to ensure that authors were adhering to the descriptive guidelines provided.

To ensure a uniform PBL learning experience for students and to assist faculty tutors who were not experts in the clinical fields represented by the cases, we requested that authors provide a brief case summary with information about the case topics, a list of 8 to 10 case objectives, and four to five references on the primary case topic. The case summary and references provided updated information about the case topic so that the non-expert tutors could better facilitate group discussion. The students were to be given the case summary and references at the end of the case to provide them with important factual information about primary case issues that they might need in the future. The case objectives were also to be given to students at the end of the case to provide a uniform learning experience. If a student group did not thoroughly discuss an objective, the students would then know that this material required review.

Some of the most annoying difficulties with the clerkship were purely logistical. While the distribution of PBL case materials to tutors appeared on the face of it to be a minor problem, tardiness in the arrival of materials promoted faculty disenchantment with the clerkship and further fostered the students' view that everything with the clerkship was disorganized. 'Faculty don't have the correct artefacts (eg x-rays) for the case' or 'faculty don't show up for their tutoring sessions' had been common student complaints. With a timeline in place to ensure that new cases would be written on schedule, I hoped that the last minute rush of case preparation would be avoided and case materials would be distributed to faculty several days before the first PBL session. Unfortunately, problems with staff support led to difficulties with clerkship activities, such as tutor assignments and room scheduling – and distribution of case materials. The Surgery Department had an office of education that had supported its third- and fourth-year clerkships for several years, but at the outset of the combined clerkship, the Medicine Department did not have staff assistance for the Internal Medicine portion of the combined clerkship. Fortunately for me, shortly after I began as the clerkship's curriculum consultant, the Department of Medicine hired an extremely competent person to function as their clerkship support staff. She quickly organized an office to accommodate the clerkship's needs and within a few weeks case distribution and other departmental communications were proceeding much more smoothly.

The scheduling of the PBL sessions for students was yet another issue to be negotiated and resolved. Medicine faculty members grumbled about the early hours for tutoring, and consultants and residents from Medicine believed students were missing important aspects of their clinical education due to their absence from morning rounds. 'They can't be full members of the team if they miss morning rounds, and the team and rounding experience are key to their learning internal medicine.' The Surgery perspective was that, given operating room demands, surgeons could serve as reliable PBL tutors only early in the morning before the operating room schedule began. While recognizing the ideal of having students from both services interact together in the PBL group, Drs Kammer, Ciproni and Grey began to realize that this goal could only be achieved at the expense of the broader goals of PBL. It was decided that the students would participate in PBL groups based on the clinical service to which they were assigned, Surgery or Medicine, and that the PBL tutor would be from the same service. Surgery students would have PBL with a Surgery tutor early in the morning, while the Medicine students would have PBL with a Medicine tutor at scheduled times in the afternoon.

What do you think of the outcome?
What other factors might have been considered, and what other options might have been tried?

CASE REPORTER'S DISCUSSION

My work with this clerkship was my first responsibility as a medical educator. It was a challenging way to start a career, but over my four and a half years with the clerkship, it became some of my most satisfying work. Dr Kammer became my mentor and encouraged me to pursue scholarly activity, and I grew professionally due to his mentoring and his 'strong personality'. By the second year of the clerkship, students were telling us that, in comparison with the other clerkships, they felt that they learnt the most on the combined Medicine/Surgery one because the clerkship activities centred on a PBL case topic each week. Drs Kammer and Grey continued to win teaching awards from the third-year students. Faculty in both departments settled down once the organizational problems were resolved, and those who participated in the clerkship's activities said that they found the activities with the students enjoyable and rewarding. Some faculty began to use the unique format of the clerkship to develop educational innovations, and scholarly work in the form of national presentations and publications resulted. For a description of the clerkship, see Blue *et al* (1996), Griffith *et al* (1995, 1996) and Schwartz *et al* (1996).

Could we have prevented the initial problems with the clerkship? In some ways, yes. First and foremost, detailed planning of the PBL cases and other clerkship activities should have occurred at the very outset. The development of case objectives, providing these objectives and other case description components to case writers, and establishing and adhering to writing timelines should have been part of the planning phase.

Second, the need for better administrative support in each of the departments for the clerkship's activities should have been anticipated. The Medical Education Office recognized that, given the extensive curriculum changes, curriculum consultants were necessary to facilitate development and implementation of educational innovations. The curriculum consultants were essential for the interdisciplinary efforts because we functioned between departments to facilitate change. While each consultant developed his or her own set of responsibilities based upon course-specific needs, we assumed responsibility for completion of tasks and projects that were not department-specific. These included the creation of syllabi, coordination of clerkship activities, facilitation of PBL case writing, PBL tutor training, monitoring of educational events and scheduling of students. However, departmental support was still required to coordinate internal communication and activities, particularly in the clerkships. The implementation of PBL does require more support than traditional lecture-based curricula and, when implemented, additional support should be forthcoming.

In other ways, perhaps the lessons learnt were unavoidable and part of the journey that all institutions must experience as part of the process of curricular change.

No one anticipated that the two clerkship directors would develop such a hostile relationship with each other. The clerkship directors were chosen because they had been the previous clerkship directors and it was just assumed they would be able to work together. The right personality mix is important when individuals are working together, particularly on a curriculum change. When possible, known personality clashes should be avoided when assigning course/clerkship directors to work together on a joint curricular change effort.

While it was known to the Medicine clerkship director at the outset of the clerkship that the timing of the early morning PBL sessions could be problematic for students on the Medicine service, substantive evidence that the timing was an impediment was not available until after the clerkship was underway – this is often the case with scheduling issues. What is important is monitoring the activity and receiving frequent feedback to determine if any problems exist. Then, when possible, schedules should be revised as soon as feasible.

The experience of working with an educational innovation that initially was poorly planned and supported has taught me the importance of good organization and sufficient support, and the value of clearly articulated course goals and objectives when initiating a course change, whether PBL is involved or not. My work with these clerkship directors also reinforced for me the need to focus on the activity at hand, not the personalities involved, in order to 'tame the lions'.

References

Blue, A, Schwartz, R and Griffith, C H III (1996) 'Development of a joint clerkship sponsored by two departments: lessons learned', *Teaching and Learning in Medicine*, 8, pp 116–23

Griffith, C H III, Blue, A V, Mainous, A G III and DeSimone, P A (1995) 'Not everybody likes problem-based learning in a clerkship', *Academic Medicine*, 70, p 660

Griffith, C H III, Blue, A V, Mainous, A G III and DeSimone, P A (1996) 'Housestaff attitudes toward a problem-based clerkship', *Medical Teacher*, 18, pp 133–34

Schwartz, R W, Blue, A V, Griffith, C H III, Felts, J and Donnelly, M B (1996) 'The structure of a combined medicine and surgery clerkship', *Medical Teacher*, 18, pp 115–18

CHAPTER 4

LOST IN THE MÊLÉE

Case reporter: D Christopher Clark

Issues raised

This case study looks at curricular reform in terms of change from a traditional lecture-based curriculum in dentistry to a 'hybrid' PBL approach. The specific issue raised is that of achieving a reduction of curricular overcrowding, which was one of the goals of moving toward PBL.

Background

The events described took place at the Faculty of Dentistry, The University of British Columbia (UBC), starting in 1994. The Faculty consists of 37 full-time faculty, about 175 undergraduate dental students, approximately 30 graduate students and a bare-bones staff support structure. Most of the faculty members are either clinical specialists or PhD trained oral biologists. The dental course is four years long.

PART 1

From 1964 to 1997, our dental students shared a traditional basic medical science curriculum with the medical students. Dentistry focused on the dental content in the first two years (especially psychomotor skills), while teaching of the basic medical sciences was left to medicine. The third and fourth years were taught entirely by dentistry. The round of curricular change began in the spring of 1994 when the Faculty of Medicine organized an internal review of its undergraduate curriculum following an accreditation visit. One of the outcomes was that, early in the autumn of 1994, the Faculty of Medicine decided to adopt a 'hybrid PBL' programme.

Although these decisions held implications for the Faculty of Dentistry, the Faculty was not consulted during the initial phases of the review or later when the Faculty of Medicine decided to develop and implement the new curriculum. Dentistry was informed of the results of the six-month process after it was completed. Medicine quickly engaged in a process of consultation and appeasement, but essentially after all the major decisions had been made.

The consequent lengthy discussions led to consensus on what dentistry could hope to accomplish through this process. The goals of the new curriculum were to:

- promote self-directed learning and problem solving;
- integrate dental and medical education;
- integrate disciplines within dentistry;
- create a rewarding learning environment;
- develop skills needed for life-long learning; and
- address problems related to the overcrowded curriculum.

The now rapidly moving set of events created high levels of turmoil and stress. We had lots to decide. What should be the level of participation of our students in the first two years of this new PBL curriculum? What will the final two years of a dental-only curriculum look like? How can we integrate dental students into a new medically-oriented curriculum where they would miss out on some of the things that had been in the traditional curriculum during years one and two? Most importantly in this respect, there would be none of the skills training that occupied so much of their time in the old pre-clinical dental curriculum. It quickly became apparent that, for this and other reasons, many faculty were opposed to the change. As might have been anticipated, without a basic understanding of PBL, many faculty reacted with opposition. Eventually, the Faculty voted almost unanimously to integrate with medicine – not because of some great love for PBL, but because we really had limited options. The Faculty of Medicine was moving ahead with or without us. Who was going to teach our students basic medical sciences?

Coincidentally, dentistry was in the process of appointing a new Dean. The process had become highly political and it fragmented the faculty. After a long and painful process, an external candidate was selected. He quickly made it clear that successful implementation of the new curriculum was his top priority. He also made it apparent that he expected the dentistry-specific years three and four to change as well. As part of his strategy, he proposed an administrative reorganization. At that time we had only three departments. The Dean's choice for a new structure was a no department model. Again the political forces surfaced and after a long process of negotiation and posturing, we arrived at a decision to have two departments instead of three!

It was a time of unbelievable stress for the Faculty – a new Dean, a new curriculum and a new administrative structure. To make things worse, all of this was happening during a time of economic downturn in British Columbia. As a result, the University budget was cut and we had few, if any, resources to support our educational efforts. We networked with PBL institutions internationally and copied and mimicked whatever we could, but it is difficult to use anyone else's materials. Ownership means doing it yourself.

There were three groups within the Faculty on whom we had to depend to do the work: 1) the oral biologists/researchers who had taught in the first two years of our old curriculum; 2) the clinical specialists who had lost teaching responsibilities in the pre-clinical course and were greatly concerned about the loss of teaching of clinical skills; and 3) the 'PBL enthusiasts', who came from a variety of disciplines, academic ranks and backgrounds. The curriculum committee hoped to bring as many faculty as possible into this last group.

The challenge was to convince sceptical faculty that this was something we could and should do. We needed their help and support. We needed them to teach in the new curriculum. We needed them to develop new teaching and learning materials. We needed them to work harder and longer, in some instances at the expense of their research interests, all for the sake of the new curriculum. We needed them to embrace the declared goals for the new curriculum.

One fact was made clear by the curriculum committee right from the start: there was no way the old content would fit into the available time in the new curriculum, despite a lengthened academic year. Besides, the goal was to decrease overcrowding of the curriculum. Most faculty started this exercise with the premise that there would be a loss of teaching time for their subject.

The questions were: How would we decide what to cut? Which objectives and activities would be eliminated? What process would be used to make these decisions? Given the political forces that had already made their presence known, how could we deal with the problem of overcrowding in the curriculum?

If you were the person(s) having to answer these questions, how would you respond?
Given the information about the participants, what do you think actually happened?

PART 2

To put it bluntly, these questions were not answered satisfactorily and our curriculum is still overcrowded. It is now the spring of 2000 and our first class of dental students is nearing completion of the new all-dental third year. On the face of it, the new third-year curriculum looks entirely different from the old one. There is only one course running at any given time, we coordinate the single course centrally and all disciplines are supposed to be integrated didactically and clinically. But despite lengthy planning, we still have an over-crowded curriculum. So, what went wrong?

We were told that support from the Dean was a prerequisite to success. We certainly would concur, and we had this. But, unfortunately, this falls short of what is really needed to 'make it happen'. Yes, the Dean's office needs to be on board. But what we did not realize we needed or necessarily get was the authority to play 'hard ball', make tough decisions and lean on some people. And this needs to happen at all administrative levels. In our case, this just did not materialize.

Because of the politics of the situation, in particular the desire of different factions to influence the decisions about time allocation in the all-dental part of the new curriculum, the Dean chaired the committee that finally handed out the time. The curriculum committee had laid out the process, goals and broad objectives of the curriculum based on our agreed-upon competencies. We tried to estimate how much time it would take students to learn their clinical skills and foundation knowledge, but the only reference for any of this was our previous experience. So this translated into a process of negotiation between the Dean and the 'content experts'.

This is when the going got tough. Far too often people were given the hours they requested (or claimed they needed) and as a result our new all-dental curriculum is overcrowded. No one is willing to give up any of his or her scheduled hours. Time is the currency of power, and the rationale is that more is better. Although curriculum time was supposed to be organized into a hybrid PBL format, we have not given students the necessary independent study time and there are more lectures than we prescribed. To a large extent, we repackaged much of the old teaching and added one PBL tutorial each week with a little independent study time. To date, we do not have enough cases to fill the new third year. We suspect that fourth year will be short of cases, too. The rest will be lectures.

Still, not everything is gloomy. On a positive note, despite the difficulties, our new PBL classes have been impressive. The students continue to perform well and it is difficult to believe that there could still be any naysayers. The students communicate well and ask so many questions, and they are so inter-ested in anything and everything. We remind our colleagues that this is why we did this; this was one of our goals. Surprisingly, some still don't make any connection between the new curriculum and how the new students perform. But to be fair, many faculty have changed their thinking after seeing the end result. We can hope that time and continued success will further influence faculty's attitudes about teaching and learning.

Are you surprised by the outcome?
What are some of the factors that may have contributed to the result?
What other options might have been tried?

CASE REPORTER'S DISCUSSION

Why did we end up with the outcome described? Why didn't the hours get cut? In the first place, the entire process was unbelievably slow and plagued by what appeared to be 'passive resistance'. People failed to come to meetings, they would leave early, or they would stall every effort to develop a final teaching schedule. During the final few months before the start of the new third year, the Dean was desperate to have a curriculum. We had not been able to get approval of a schedule that satisfied everyone and we had no more time to convince people that they should use PBL. In the end, faculty worried that the students wouldn't learn the material unless it was given to them. The prevailing thought seemed to be: ' PBL is a good teaching method for everyone but me. My stuff is different.' So faculty did what they thought they needed to do. They negotiated for the hours they needed with little consideration of the PBL. In the end, faculty had the time they wanted to teach the way they always had.

Compromises resulted in the loss of many of the potential advantages of PBL. Our students are now in a longer, overcrowded curriculum with a little PBL. In theory, people knew what was expected in terms of the curriculum plan, but there was little incentive to actually redevelop or rethink the curriculum, and there were no negative consequences if faculty refused to cooperate. In reality, most of our teachers seem to have little faith that our students can make good decisions about what and how to learn. Essentially, many faculty do not seem to accept the tenets of PBL, especially when it comes to their own content. Despite all the faculty development, faculty still hold reasonably archaic views about how students learn.

In our particular situation, what hurt us most was attitude. Some faculty hold a narrow view of their role as 'teacher': the expert delivering content to students – and the more content, the better. This view is justified with statements like: 'But they need this foundation knowledge'. Opponents of PBL continue to worry about possible gaps in students' knowledge while ignoring the obvious similar gaps that occur with traditional teaching methods – even when comprehensive 'coverage' is claimed.

Perhaps most disappointing was the fact that some senior administrators felt unwilling or unable to fight for an integrated and interactive new curriculum. They had the power and influence, but they rarely used it to help the initiative. In their defence, when change is necessary and resistance is met, the traditional academic system usually has limited power to influence what people do.

What is needed during the planning and implementation of an innovative learning environment such as PBL is effective control over the process. It requires an interdisciplinary approach that neutralizes the vested interests of specialists or disciplines that fail to share the institutional vision. No individual concern should be allowed to interfere with the institutional mission.

I believe that a widely representative group of faculty needs to plan, develop and implement the curriculum. This group cannot be self-selected, but it should be a representative selection of people who are interested and who are acknowledged as interested and committed teachers. Senior faculty are key players in this equation and they can make or break the effort. If curricular change is truly desired, decisions cannot be made in the absence of a shared and common vision.

So far, this discussion has consisted of the reflections of someone who has been closely involved with the change to the dental curriculum – and who has been disappointed in many aspects of the outcome. It has also looked at individual parts of the picture. Considered more dispassionately and from a more global perspective, what other reasons might be cited for the difficulties we experienced?

In essence, our situation illustrates the tension between administrative force on the one hand and popular support and ownership on the other in securing major curricular change. Which is more likely to be effective, the 'power' position of 'top down' enforcement of change or the 'bottom up' strategy of winning people over? Ideally, support should come from both directions, but examples could be given where the driving force has come from above and others where it has come from below. Some influential writers, such as Abrahamson (1998), suggest that the Dean's role is vital. But is it really true that more 'push' by senior administrators would see PBL successfully introduced and prospering? If faculty do not want it to work, would they find ways to sabotage it anyway? Would senior administrators find it easier and more acceptable to make tough decisions if more work has first been put into developing/bringing along/'capturing' faculty?

In any event, the saving grace in all of this and the justification for continuing to try to reduce the overloading in the curriculum is the response of the students to PBL. In our experience, and despite the problems, the integration of dental students into the first two years of basic medical sciences at UBC should be viewed as a success. Although we have had little or no time to do research on our educational experiment, almost everyone is impressed with our students. They are different from the students in the old curriculum. They ask a lot of questions. They probably think better and they definitely communicate better. Do they know more, are their clinical skills up to par and will they make better dentists? I have no answers to these questions, unfortunately. It will take dentistry years, maybe decades, to learn about the outcomes of PBL. But for UBC, even though we probably did not do it very well, I doubt that we will ever go back. I don't think that we will return to a completely lecture-based curriculum. Our students probably would not tolerate a passive environment after having experienced something like PBL. Besides, enough of us faculty have seen the light.

Reference

Abrahamson, S (1998) 'Obstacles to establishing problem-based learning', *Journal of Dental Education*, **62**, pp 656–59

CHAPTER 5

BUT WHAT IF THEY LEAVE WITH MISINFORMATION?

Case reporter: Gwendie Camp

Issues raised

This case study illustrates a common concern of both faculty and students when they are contemplating the adoption of PBL. They are often overly concerned that students will leave a PBL group with misinformation because someone, usually a fellow student, has offered inaccurate information that has not been corrected by either the faculty facilitator or by other students.

Background

The events described took place at the University of Texas Medical Branch (UTMB), a large, public medical school and the oldest medical school in Texas. At the time this concern was expressed most often and most openly (the late 1990s), the UTMB faculty was considering making large changes to its traditional curriculum. The School had, for several years, a parallel 'pure' problem-based track for a small group of students (24 per year). The remainder of the class (approximately 180 students) was in the 'traditional' curriculum. The total number of faculty was nearly 900, although fewer than 200 had any regular involvement in the curriculum of Years 1 and 2, and fewer than 50 had had any involvement with the problem-based curriculum track.

PART 1

The Dean of UTMB had recently come from another medical school that had converted from a traditional curriculum to a 'hybrid' PBL curriculum. He was convinced that PBL was the appropriate direction for the UTMB curriculum to take. He began a process of curriculum change by appointing a series of 'design' committees, each charged with making recommendations regarding changes to the curriculum. All of the design committees, each made up of about 12 faculty members plus a member of the Office of Educational Development, had a 'progressive' flavour, although 'old guard' or healthy sceptics were also included on each committee.

It was clear early in the deliberations that PBL was going to be one of several key components of the redesigned curriculum. While the School had had a parallel 'pure' problem-based track for about two years at the time of the design teamwork, only about 50 faculty members (at most) had direct (and positive) experience with the PBL track. However, many of the faculty had lined up against PBL, for a variety of reasons. One of the opponents was a highly respected senior member of the Anatomy Department and a highly acclaimed teacher. His basic view of education was the classical model, with the teacher as the 'expert' delivering content in a caring, yet rigorous, way to eager students. He had no experience with any other model.

As one device for involving the whole faculty (or as many as could be bothered) in the process of curriculum change, the Dean initiated a series of 'faculty forums'. At each meeting, the Dean updated the faculty attendees with the reports of the design committees and opened the floor to questions and comments. At the very first of these faculty forums, Colin, the respected Anatomy teacher, was quick to comment and ask a question.

'I've been willing to work on reorganizing the content of our curriculum and to make recommendations about what content should be included at the beginning of the curriculum in a "basic science core", but I'm not at all happy about this proposal that we incorporate problem-based learning small groups with cases instead of experts giving lectures on the required material. You tell me that the students will learn on their own and that the facilitators (we don't even pretend to call them teachers) don't have to know the content themselves. But what if a student says something that is incorrect – and you know one of them will – and the teacher, excuse me, facilitator, doesn't correct it? They'll leave with misinformation. And they'll never even know it. This is abdicating our responsibility as a faculty. It's our job to see to it that students get accurate, up-to-date information, not misinformation.'

The Dean looked at me expectantly, so I rose to respond. But what would be the best way to respond to concerns like Colin's?

If you were the one expected to respond to Colin's statement, what would you say?
What other actions would you suggest for later?

PART 2

Given the constraints of time and place, I confined myself to a brief response. I said, 'I'll admit that it is possible that the scenario you've painted could happen. But in tutorial groups that are running well, students challenge each other and the facilitator doesn't have to be the one to correct misperceptions. Besides, we know that in our traditional curriculum lots of students leave courses with incorrect information, because they don't all make perfect scores on our tests.'

The meeting proceeded on to other issues, but Colin was clearly not persuaded. After the forum, he met up with me and said, 'You're going to have to do better than that'.

The Dean had another strategy for dealing with Colin. He appointed him as head of the design team for the 'Basic Science Core', which turned out later to be the first 24 weeks of the curriculum. The design teams began to meet in earnest, once a week. Colin and his group had a difficult time at first. Colin was very worried that 'trendy' educational ideas would cause the deterioration of content learning in favour of 'fun'.

One of my colleagues (another Assistant Dean and one of the leaders of the PBL track) then suggested to students in the PBL track that they ask Colin (Dr Duncan to them) to give a 'correlate' on some aspect of anatomy. In our PBL track, a 'correlate' is an interactive lecture requested by students because of difficulties they are encountering in their learning by other methods. The students asked and Colin agreed, mainly because he is a dedicated teacher and cannot resist eager learners. To his surprise, he was quite impressed by the students' enthusiasm and motivation for learning. But he still wasn't convinced that they had mastered the content (after all, not all students attended the 'correlated session'). As luck would have it, Colin recounted his experiences with the PBL-track students to his design team, and, even luckier, the director of the PBL track was a member of the same team. The Director challenged Colin to go even further: to actually be a facilitator for the up-coming block. He promised Colin that he would not have the same attitude at the end of the eight weeks.

Colin did become a facilitator and he had a complete change of heart about problem-based learning as a result of his interactions with the students over the eight weeks, plus their performance on the end-of-block assessments. He became a champion of the new curriculum, going so far as to suggest that the new curriculum should not be a 'hybrid' but should be completely problem based. And, most significantly, he said that he now saw how a group of learners could be intellectually honest with each other, questioning one another's assertions, assessing the quality of learning resources, and admitting when they were wrong or did not know the answer.

Although we didn't have another conversation about the issue of misinformation, he never again seemed worried that PBL students would be at a disadvantage because they didn't have a content expert present in their tutorial groups to correct any content mistakes. I suppose I should have put the question back to him: 'But what if they leave with misinformation?' It would have been interesting to hear his response!

As an epilogue, Colin was later elected to the Curriculum Committee by the faculty, primarily based on his past position as a strong basic scientist and his strong opinions about classical teaching. However, after his experiences with the PBL track, he was also a strong advocate for appropriate implementation of the new curriculum with its backbone of PBL.

What do you think of the strategies used by the Assistant Dean and the PBL Director?
What would you have done differently?
What other methods might be used to convince sceptics?

CASE REPORTER'S DISCUSSION

This case illustrates the point that 'engaging' or enlisting the naysayers can be very effective, especially if they are open-minded enough to get involved. If the naysayer is interested in teaching, though, and often such people are, then he or she may be willing to try out the new method at least to prove that it isn't as good as the old way. Sometimes one experience is not enough. In Colin's case, giving a single 'correlate' was not sufficient to allay his concerns, but the students' enthusiasm and motivation were positive features of the PBL curriculum that intrigued him – enough so that when he was 'challenged' to tutor, he agreed. You might call this stepwise strategy 'softening him up by stages'.

It was interesting to see the effects of the PBL-track students' interactions with Colin. By and large, they were very positive in both directions: on the students, as Colin showed the same kind of enthusiasm for teaching students (and learning from them) as he had always shown – and most importantly on Colin in contributing to his 'conversion'. As in many other instances, it can be the students and their shared learning experiences with the faculty member that make the critical difference in changing the mind of a sceptical teacher.

Converts often make some of the most powerful spokespersons for an innovation. The proponents of the 'old way' see them as being more discriminating, more demanding of good data and more sensible than the 'firebrands' who initiated the innovation. They then can be very effective in bringing some of their old allies into the new order.

With regard to the original theme of this case, the direct experience of working with students engaged in PBL was the best (and possibly the only) way to convince someone like Colin that the original assertion about students correcting their own information during PBL sessions was true. No amount of intellectual or theoretical argument or quotation of others' experiences would have worked.

In this instance, it was his own experience of what happened in PBL sessions that convinced Colin. Had there been the opportunity, it might also have been useful for Colin to be made aware of some of the theoretical issues surrounding the question of students obtaining 'misinformation' from PBL sessions. For example, he could have been reminded of the 'iterative' nature of knowledge – the fact that we visit and revisit concepts many times, form new relationships among them, develop new links, gain new insights and intuitions, new perspectives, different frames, different interpretive possibilities. That is how real learning occurs. The notion that a single piece of information is obtained one time – and that it then stays forever – is for the most part unsupportable. Also, what is 'incorrect' information? Any two academics in a single discussion are liable to disagree about many things. Who is 'right'? The important issue is not 'having' wrong information but having the orientation to constantly develop and improve one's knowledge – and this is exactly what PBL encourages.

CHAPTER 6

MIXED MODELS AND MIXED MESSAGES

Case reporters: Marilyn S Lantz and John F Chaves

Issues raised

This case study focuses on the challenges facing those who implement PBL programmes during periods of administrative transition and the challenges facing students as they cope with a new curriculum in which some, but not all, courses use PBL.

Background

Indiana University School of Dentistry (IUSD) offers a four-year programme leading to the award of the DDS (Doctor of Dental Surgery) degree. Prior to 1997, the School offered a traditional DDS programme, the first two years of which consisted mostly of biomedical and pre-clinical dental sciences courses delivered mainly through traditional lecture and laboratory courses. Some lecture-based courses and seminars were included in the third and fourth years of the programme, but mainly third- and fourth-year students provide comprehensive patient care in the School's dental clinics. Approximately 130 full-time and 110 part-time faculty members provide instruction for a total of 400 dental students – about 100 students per class. In 1997, IUSD started a new DDS programme in which problem-based learning was the major instructional approach for the courses offered by the Department of Oral Biology (one of IUSD's five departments).

PART 1

During the early to mid-1990s, IUSD experienced a turbulent interval of curriculum development. The Dean, who had championed curriculum reform, resigned in 1996 and was replaced by an Acting Dean. A new Dean was recruited and assumed administrative responsibility in January 1997. Centralized administrative structures that should have evolved to support the planned curriculum changes, such as an Office of Education headed by an Associate Dean, had failed to develop. Eventually, the responsibility for curriculum improvement was vested in departments after rejection by faculty of a blueprint for a new DDS curriculum that had been prepared by a faculty-wide committee. In mid-1996, a new proposal for remodelling the DDS programme was approved by the faculty, with implementation scheduled for the class entering in the summer of 1997. Components of this proposal were based firmly on departmental initiatives.

For its contribution to the new curriculum, the Department of Oral Biology developed a series of four sequential integrated courses to deliver the major biomedical and behavioural sciences offerings for the first two years of the DDS programme. Ours was the only department that chose to use PBL as a major instructional mode for our new courses.

The Department ran its first month-long PBL pilot course in July 1996. This pilot course, entitled 'Introduction to Critical Thinking and Professional Behaviour', for which the two of us served as course directors, was well received by both the students and the faculty who served as tutors. It gave us an indication of the huge amount of work that would be involved for the Department during the full curriculum, as the Department would be responsible for both the administrative and the academic aspects of running the PBL courses.

The first class of students in the new curriculum arrived at IUSD on 1 July 1997. For one month they took our department's introductory course ('Introduction to Critical Thinking and Professional Behaviour'), based on the previous year's pilot course, designed to give them an orientation to the professional role and to 'learning how to learn' in the PBL courses. They also had the opportunity to practice functioning in tutorial groups. This course, like the pilot course the previous year, was well received by both the students and the faculty members who served as tutors. However, student concerns regarding some of the new methods of instruction and of assessment developed within weeks after the introductory course ended and the three first-semester courses began.

Although there were teething problems affecting the new DDS programme as a whole, additional problems plagued our own department's PBL courses. First, the tutors, who were drawn from all departments of the School, were not adequately trained for consistency in assessing student performance in tutorials or in the assessment which tested students' use of the PBL process (the 'triple-jump' examination, developed at McMaster University). Moreover, some of the tutors lacked the skills to keep 'stalled' groups moving forward and to help 'problem' groups in general. As a result, it became common knowledge that some tutorial groups consistently had brief sessions, with predictable impact on the motivation and morale of other groups and tutors. While the Oral Biology Department was aware of these problems, its limited resources were fully consumed just keeping its part of the programme going. Moreover, it had limited formal authority to rectify problems involving staff from other departments.

We were also plagued with technical problems, some avoidable, others not. Some tutors had outdated computers with such limited system resources that their ability to use Web-based tools was severely impaired. On two occasions, a lack of allocated space on the server prevented completed assessments from being submitted, requiring them to be re-done a week later. These sorts of technical problems led to anger and frustration which was directed towards us in the Department of Oral Biology even when the problems were beyond our control. Against this backdrop, the directors of the PBL courses were trying to 'enculturate' students to new sets of skills and behaviours. First, the PBL courses required students to function in a highly independent manner as learners and to set their own learning agenda in tutorial groups. Second, students experiencing difficulty, either in tutorials or on examinations, were asked initially to self-identify. In addition, students who wished to review their performance on biweekly examinations were required to come to the department office to review them. This system was put in place so that we could monitor the effects on student performance of a variety of new interventions for helping students who were experiencing difficulty.

Given the problems with the courses, the new responsibilities being placed on the students, and the fact that ours was the only department using such a new and unfamiliar teaching method, it was little wonder that some of the students reacted negatively. The students who were experiencing the most difficulty were the least likely to seek help. Some students reacted angrily to the inconvenience of having to come to the department office to review their examinations, preferring instead the familiar convenience of having examinations returned to them. Others were troubled by our decision to allow the students to play a small but direct role in determining their own grades in tutorials through self- and peer-assessment.

The PBL course directors had anticipated that some students would experience difficulty adjusting to the new expectations for their attitudes, behaviours and performance. They crafted a formal system for getting regular feedback from students that could be anonymous if the student desired. Students were encouraged to express their concerns orally or in writing to their tutors and their advisers. Course directors met regularly with class officers to discuss student concerns and transmit information. Students were encouraged to bring concerns to the course and module directors. In addition, the course directors met with the class as a whole three times during the semester. Finally, students regularly completed course and faculty evaluations. The goal of the formal feedback system was to allow students to voice their concerns responsibly to the individuals who could best help to resolve them. With all of these mechanisms in place, we felt that we were ready to deal with any difficulty students were having with the new courses. However, things didn't work out as we had planned.

Many of the students had friends and/or relatives who were still in the 'old' programme, ie the later years of the curriculum. In spite of our efforts to introduce a new 'culture' into the entering class, many of the students' expectations for what dental school should be like were heavily shaped by what the students in the later years told them about 'how things should be' in dental school. The culture of the old programme was also reinforced by some of the faculty. Some of these faculty members retained a strong commitment to discipline-based teaching. For example, at orientation for the new class, the director of one of the three first-semester courses announced: 'I'm from the department that really teaches you how to be a dentist!' In addition, a few very vocal faculty members were outspokenly critical of the PBL approach and felt that the new programme overall contained 'too damn much science'. They did not mind sharing their views openly with the students. This overt dissension served to amplify and validate any and all student discontent with the PBL courses. Moreover, some of the unhappy students were the children of IUSD alumni and on at least one occasion a couple of these alumni parents came to the dental school to discuss their concerns with the Dean.

Understandably, some administrators were disturbed by what they were hearing and they began to hold meetings with students to discuss their concerns about the new curriculum. Meanwhile, the mechanisms that we had carefully constructed to deal with students' concerns stood waiting to be utilized.

We were eventually asked to meet with the Dean and the Associate Dean for Academic Affairs. At this meeting, one of them told us: 'The students are uncomfortable with your portion of the programme'. Our assessment methods and tools were said to be 'too sophisticated' and 'they take too long to complete'. Some of our alumni (parents) were angry and it was reported that some said: 'This new programme is a terrible break with IUSD's traditions'. Finally we were asked: 'Why don't you return all examinations to the students as soon as they're graded, as the students want, rather than forcing them to come to the department to go over them?' The profound communication gap that was revealed and the resulting intensity of the negative reaction astonished us. This had obviously developed into a real crisis. How had it happened and how should we deal with it?

What factors contributed to the development of this situation?
If you were faced with this situation, what would you do next?
What do you think actually was done and how did it turn out?

PART 2

We recognized that at least some of the reactions displayed by the students were their response to uncertainty and lack of agreement about the new programme among us, other faculty, and the administration – and that a part of this was due to inadequate communication. During the rest of our meeting with the Dean and Associate Dean and at a subsequent meeting, we first attempted to get more information about the administration's concerns. We then presented the pedagogical and logistical issues from our perspective and described our formal system for obtaining and addressing student concerns. We suggested that, when such a system is bypassed, the individuals most able to correct problems are unaware even that the problems exist. Besides, in our view, students' initial discomfort with many aspects of PBL is expected and can be adaptive, serving as an important source of motivation for the complex shift from teacher-centred to student-centred learning. Finally, we attempted to clarify the formative role that assessment is expected to play in our programme. That role was an important rationale for the methods and tools we had employed.

After negotiation, the administration agreed to meet with only those students who had exhausted the formal process for expressing concerns and whose concerns remained unaddressed. They also agreed to let us know when they were meeting with students. For our part, we agreed to meet with the administration and update them regarding student concerns and our efforts to address them.

The administration issued a formal statement, asking faculty who did not agree with the PBL philosophy to refrain from sharing their views with the students. Subsequently, the formal system for dealing with students' concerns worked effectively and their frequency and severity decreased markedly. While this immediate crisis was dealt with successfully, we were sensitized to the longer-term need to maintain good relations and lines of communication with other faculty and with the administration and to have the best possible level of organization for our own courses. Only then could we hope that the messages students were receiving about our portion of the programme would be consistent – and positive!

What do you think of the outcome?
What other measures might have been tried?

CASE REPORTERS' DISCUSSION

The implementation of our new DDS programme was problematic for our students, our faculty and our administration alike. The faculty was highly polarized in its views about the new programme. This was one consequence of the fact that the new curriculum was developed largely along departmental lines, without a unifying shared vision for its outcomes among the faculty as a whole. As a result, students received mixed messages from the faculty about what skills, attitudes and behaviours are desired in our programme. For example, including both traditional and PBL courses in our DDS programme required students to regularly 'switch gears' between courses in which faculty-centred learning was the norm and those in which student-centred learning was the norm. Success in these two types of course requires very different skills, behaviours and attitudes. Our sense is that under these conditions, some students retreated into an academic survival mode and behaved in ways our programme was not designed to promote.

Similarly, the faculty who developed the PBL portion of the new programme faced a very difficult situation. Development of this portion of the programme was strongly supported by the former Dean, who had made a commitment to the PBL course directors to set up an appropriate centralized administrative structure to support this new learning strategy. All of our plans for this programme were predicated on the assumption that such a system would be in place before the implementation of the new DDS programme. Six months before full implementation of the new programme, and after three years of planning and development by the Department, a new Dean arrived at the School. His vision for supporting the PBL component of the new DDS programme differed considerably from the one that had been developed by the previous Dean and the course directors. The new Dean also had a difficult task. He entered a contentious and highly charged political environment and had to consider the needs of the whole school and the DDS programme in making decisions about support.

While some of the difficulties we experienced were beyond anyone's control, we believe there are lessons to be learnt from these experiences that may be useful to others. It would have been extremely helpful if more had been done to anticipate and deal with the institutional cultural issues that divided the faculty. The faculty needed to be able to articulate a clear and shared vision for the outcomes of the educational programmes. In turn, that requires some agreement about the nature of the problems faced by the dental profession, dental education and the academic health centres in which dental schools are generally housed. A recent study by the National Academy of Sciences, 'Dental Education at the Crossroads', has addressed many of these concerns, but a consensus still seems to be lacking among faculty.

Many of the problems that we confronted also seem traceable to the difficulty in comprehending the fundamental nature of the paradigm shift that is implied by a change to a PBL curriculum. Often, participants (students, faculty and administrators) seem to view PBL as simply an alternative teaching method to deliver traditional curricular content. Successful transition to a PBL curriculum, in our view, requires that all participants come to understand the fundamental changes that are required in our assumptions about the nature of knowledge as well as the nature of teaching and learning.

For faculty, the challenge is to define strategies by which various disciplines can share teaching/learning methods that value discovery learning, the acquisition of self-assessment skills and the integration of knowledge across traditional disciplinary boundaries. Also required is a new approach to assessment that emphasizes its formative dimensions and the need for its seamless integration into the teaching process.

We must also appreciate that, for students, becoming socialized into PBL may involve a lengthy process during which they may well feel some discomfort. Resistance during this phase is to be expected, but it should not be used as a rationale for bypassing the structures and processes used to support PBL. We need to understand the reasons why students may be uncomfortable and support them in ways that are consistent with the educational values that are implicit in PBL approaches.

Finally, in addition to all of the factors described above, we must also consider whether some modification of our course structures might have served everyone better. This is certainly a fair question and at first blush might prompt a resounding 'yes!' It is clearly in everyone's interest to have all of the important stakeholders on board, particularly the students! On further reflection, however, the 'best solution' becomes less clear. At the heart of this matter is a concern that will arise for all new PBL programmes, particularly hybrid ones in which a portion of the curriculum continues to be delivered in a traditional format. How much can a PBL programme deviate from the tenets of problem-based learning and still call itself a 'PBL programme'? There was tremendous pressure on us from all stakeholders to revise our departmental courses in ways that would have re-established more traditional faculty/student roles. While making accommodations that would have reduced student autonomy and accountability and would have yielded short-term relief was a possibility, we were concerned that the cost to the students and our programme over the long run might have been too high. Throughout the first semester we struggled to balance our obligation to generate an evidentiary base from which to make future decisions about programmatic changes with our obligation to meet the real and perceived needs of our students. How could we insist that our students learn to practice evidence-based dentistry if we were not committed to practicing evidence-based dental education?

The Russian cognitive psychologist Lev Vygotsky noted that at any point in development, there are certain problems that the learner is just on the verge of being able to solve – with assistance. He referred to this part of the problem spectrum as the zone of proximal development. More complex problems, outside of this zone, remain insoluble, even with assistance. Similarly, as institutions develop, they also have their zones of proximal development. The challenge for educational change agents is to both recognize those limits and fashion innovations that are consistent with them, while preserving the integrity of the educational approach they are advocating.

CHAPTER 7

OVERCOMING OBSTACLES

Case reporter: Ann Sefton

Issues raised

This case explores two of the difficulties commonly encountered when well-established, traditional institutions are engaged in major reform of the medical curriculum. They concern the problems of juggling the simultaneous planning of many interrelated aspects of curriculum change and the challenges of over-coming the dissension arising from a need for integration. In particular, this case addresses the challenges of achieving a vertically integrated curriculum when the organizational model is horizontal (ie in the form of departments).

Background

The University of Sydney Medical School first enrolled students in 1883. Until recently, it admitted the majority of each class directly from secondary school into a five- or six-year curriculum. The traditional discipline-based programme progressed from basic science through the medical sciences with the students full-time in clinical studies only in the fourth year, after some very limited exposure to patients in the third year. Class sizes are over 200. The Faculty of Medicine is distributed widely geographically not only on the University's main campus, but also in four clinical schools that incorporate six major and many minor and specialist teaching hospitals, up to 300 kilometres away.

PART 1

By 1990, I had been a neuroscientist in the Department of Physiology at Sydney and a Sub-Dean for pre-clinical students for over 25 years. Since my medical student days, I have been actively involved in educational issues and classroom innovation, trying to improve the quality of the education that I – and students since – had been subjected to. The situation at Sydney reflected many of the universal concerns about traditional medical education. Our curriculum was massively bloated since older content was never pruned. Increasingly esoteric topics within existing disciplines were added, while new areas outside traditional departmental responsibilities were almost impossible to include, or were introduced at basic levels multiple times. The hugely inflated, so-called essential 'core' curriculum seemed to be built on the assumption that students stopped learning on graduation. Further, the content was not integrated or even vaguely coordinated in any way, either within or between years, so that students had no sense of progressive development in either skills or knowledge.

In fact, the 'empty vessel' model of education prevailed: in didactic classes, passive heads were 'filled' with isolated facts and students were rewarded for recalling them. Students thus saw surface learning as essential for survival. Information was presented in a fragmentary way within rigid discipline boundaries. Clinical experience was delayed and initially introduced only in a token fashion. It was thus hardly surprising that students had little confidence in reasoning clinically, applying their knowledge or making informed medical decisions. We did not encourage the systematic use of information technology for diagnostic data gathering, patient management, and evidence-based practice or even as a learning tool. Most students had recognized and reported these deficiencies for years. Many found the lack of real intellectual challenge disappointing and engaged in a variety of displacement activities. Their commitment to the programme, even to clinical activities, was poor.

In response to such concerns, we attempted reform during the mid-1970s (a five-year curriculum) and the mid-1980s (with a return to six years). Although actively involved, as a junior staff member I was powerless to influence the big picture but did contribute to isolated elements (eg integrated neuroscience). Some of us soon realized that the resultant hard-won changes were essentially ineffective; they had been based on preserving relative time allocations that maintained historical departmental autonomy. In particular, while we wrote lofty statements of aims for both curricula, they were prepared independently, after the plans were completed. The goals thus bore no relation to the actual curriculum.

As if that were not enough, in the late 1980s yet another attempt was launched, to define the 'vertical' curriculum by mapping the contributions of departments to disciplines based on body systems. Redundancies and significant gaps were identified, but the three of us responsible soon realized that such helpful vertical structures could not be imposed effectively on a horizontally organized departmental model. The Faculty also bravely passed a resolution that its curriculum committee should have 'teeth', but departmental power and the governance structures made any centralized control impossible.

Another critical issue for us at the time was student selection. Most students entered medicine at Sydney from amongst the highest performing 0.5 per cent on state examinations. They often had no clinical motivation and indeed knew little about medical careers. Pressured by parents and schools, they opted 'not to waste' their excellent grades by enrolling in university courses of lower prestige in which they were actually more interested. Performance in English did not contribute to selection, and the poor communication skills of some students were quite rightly concerning academics, patients, the profession and hospital administrators alike. Many staff were muttering darkly about changing selection criteria, some favouring the entry of graduates and others a combined degree structure with medical sciences.

The Dean generated Faculty-wide discussion of these issues by hosting meetings with each department during 1991. By then Associate Dean, and newly returned from the Harvard New Pathway Program, I attended them all, introducing the issues and making the case for educational change. Realizing that I was 'going out on a limb', I none the less considered the potential end result worth the risk. The Dean was able to maintain judicious neutrality.

Views diverged widely. Some vocal and dominant radicals had an overt agenda to ensure early career specialization. Others – more discreetly – sought to increase the fraction of the curriculum devoted to their own 'essential' discipline, to ensure its continuing survival. Yet others reasonably hoped to introduce or expand under-represented areas (eg molecular biology, evidence-based medicine, community health), or emphasized the need for new educational processes. Fortunately, at least some were sufficiently altruistic to support balanced, rational, evidence-based educational change. Reform looked as though it just might be achievable.

A crucial Faculty meeting was held in October 1991. At it, some were vocally opposed to any reconsideration of the curriculum whatsoever. The complacent pointed to Sydney's longstanding high reputation for producing good graduates, ignoring the students' persistent criticisms of their educational experiences. The conservatives recited like parrots the hackneyed phrase 'if it ain't broke, don't fix it', an unsustainable proposition in the face of growing evidence that the curriculum was indeed 'broke'. The cautious waited to see. The cynics, some scarred by previous unsuccessful attempts, doubted that Faculty could or would carry it through.

It was thus impossible to estimate the strength of support. Given our depressing history, even the well disposed had no faith that anything would ever happen and were exhausted from previous attempts. I knew, too, that there was absolutely no agreement on single reform solutions for either curriculum or selection.

At the meeting, the debate indicated that, indeed, a majority accepted the need for some re-thinking (tinged with resignation – 'not again?'). The meeting agreed to investigate change for one year, before making a final decision on the basis of a summary report. When the initial relief and surprise subsided, I was ecstatic! This was *the* chance not to be missed.

We now needed to determine the strategies for planning so we could present a 'once and for all' report to Faculty in one year's time. By then, a consensus had to be forged, and the brief was nothing less than to change radically an entire curriculum. From the discussions already held, the overall direction of change was clearly to be to a more student-centred approach, an integrated curriculum that would replace a subject-based one, a greater emphasis on critical reasoning and learning skills, and the replacement of an academic method of student selection by a more targeted process to match the new educational strategies. But how best could we achieve these goals?

If you were in the position of the case reporter and had overall responsibility for the initial and later processes, would you have managed the early steps differently? If so, in what way? What were the strengths and weaknesses in the approach taken by the Dean?
What methods would you recommend for taking the process further? What strategies would ensure both wide consultation and effective decision making?

PART 2

Immediately after the meeting, I felt a succession of emotions, not the least being awe at the magnitude of the task we were confronting. The whole body of interlocking issues of curriculum seemed amorphous and impenetrable. Our previous experiences represented an awful portent of failure.

The Dean asked me to chair a small Steering Committee that would consist of me, two experienced and supportive members of Faculty, and the Chairs of the five groups that were to work for one year to investigate details, consult widely (including a major workshop for each group) and prepare reports so that Faculty could make informed decisions on whether to change and what 'shape' any change might take. The groups were to: set goals for any new programme; outline a curriculum; consider principles of assessment; suggest admission strategies; and – somewhat unrelated – plan the development of four clinical schools from the myriad of Faculty's clinical teaching sites. We encouraged academic and clinical staff as well as students to join any committee of interest; in the event, about 120 did so. The participation of students in particular was wholehearted and altruistic, especially considering that we were looking to replace the programme that was the basis of their degree.

In a moment of excessive zeal, I also agreed to chair the Curriculum planning group. To encourage coordination between the groups, I attended virtually all the different meetings. The extent of my commitment forced me to make hard decisions about other priorities. It was a busy time!

Emotionally, it had all the characteristics of a roller coaster: from elation at small hints of progress to despair when consensus eluded us.

The committees needed to work in parallel, although their work was interdependent. For example, the goals at graduation needed to be matched with appropriate educational processes and strategies. The recommendations on prerequisite knowledge and skills, related to selection of university graduates or those who had just completed secondary school (the 'hottest' issue in our context), would profoundly affect curriculum content, emphasis and duration. Assessment principles needed to be consistent with the as-yet-undecided goals and curriculum strategies.

The crucial Goals group, chaired by a key public health academic, proved the most controversial as it strove to determine the philosophy and values for a new curriculum. Consensus proved elusive as the conservatives and the complacent battled the various flavours of radicals while the cautious and the cynics held their fire.

Within the Curriculum group, some expressed enthusiasm to embrace curricular change, but by no means was everyone committed. Attendance was erratic so that previous discussions were repeatedly rehashed with a shifting population. To my frustration, few were willing to speculate or develop possibilities in the absence of direction from agreed goals. This lack of progress itself discouraged all but the most enthusiastic from attending regularly. To make matters worse, one senior professor of a pre-clinical discipline – a major researcher – argued trenchantly and repeatedly (with the aid of some rather dated references) that the basis for all medical knowledge lay in the powerful disciplinary structures established last century. In his view, any hint of integration would threaten the very basis of modern medicine and distort students' understanding. In particular, he emphasized that his own discipline – 'central to medicine' – must be maintained intact. He conveyed an air of lofty academic righteousness and I felt helpless.

At the first Faculty-wide workshop – on goals – antagonistic and confrontational views were expressed. Critical issues included generalist vs specialist emphasis, the extent to which a community focus was appropriate, and the relative importance of more generic academic, learning and reasoning skills compared with specific scientific or clinical knowledge and skills. After much heated discussion, it was accepted, often grudgingly, that Australian medical graduates must continue to be prepared as generalists, not specialists. The long traditions of the School, however, ensured that we would still strive to produce high quality, enthusiastic researchers, teachers, specialists and public health practitioners – 'hedging our bets'.

We knew from previous experience that our departmental organization was inappropriate for generating an integrated curriculum. A major breakthrough occurred from an interchange between the Goals and Curriculum groups when a thematic approach was proposed and adopted. Ultimately, four themes (Basic and Clinical Science, Patient and Doctor, Community and

Doctor, Personal and Professional Development) were defined. They provided the necessary interdisciplinary framework for the new curriculum both to organize the goals and to serve as progressive 'strands' continuing throughout the entire programme.

Unfortunately, that simple solution failed to stifle the arguments about retaining discipline-based learning. I produced relevant literature on the educational issues and the power of integration in medical programmes. Others referred to successful problem-based programmes they had visited, while a few conservatives (including our friend, the professor) continued to argue that the disciplines had, after all, served us well, and produced more dated philosophical articles in support.

In desperation to break the logjam, and anxious to determine the real views and depth of feeling, I devised a short questionnaire for the members of the Curriculum group. Should the programme be discipline-based or integrated? If integrated, were the four themes an appropriate framework? If so, what should be the weighting of each theme? To what extent was problem-based learning supported? Was there a commitment to early clinical experience?

Virtually every member responded. Only one (guess who?) preferred a discipline-based curriculum; everyone else supported integration. They overwhelmingly endorsed the theme-based structure. A substantial majority opted for introducing problem-based learning. All endorsed early clinical experience. Around this time it became apparent that the Admissions group would most likely recommend graduate entry and a four-year programme. Discussion then proceeded apace and a curriculum was outlined; it received favourable support from respected visiting medical educators.

At a historic meeting at the end of the year of initial planning, the decision was made resoundingly to move to a four-year, problem-based programme: 166 in favour and six against. The final report to Faculty from all of the groups represented a blueprint for implementation, albeit with minor modifications and enhancements. Unexpectedly, perhaps the easiest decision was the one to embark on graduate entry.

What do you see as the key strategies that worked? Could they have been done differently or more efficiently?
Were there strategies that failed or things that could have been done better?

CASE REPORTER'S DISCUSSION

On reflection, the commitment to change proved stronger than either the Dean or I had anticipated. The climate of criticism of traditional medical education overseas was helpful. Support from significant medical educators can only help. The postponement of the final decision to allow wide discussion for a year was crucial in the final successful outcome: faculty now had a clear blueprint to consider. The curriculum outline, educational processes, admissions, assessment and the clinical developments were all consistent with the overall goals and principles. Thus the separation of the initial planning from later implementation was a powerful strategy.

There were, I believe, two real turning points during the planning discussions. First was the hard-won agreement on the goals of the new curriculum, from which flowed a number of implicit consequences. The second was the realization that the opponents of integration were relatively few in number, albeit influential, while the supporters were many and enthusiastic.

The Dean's support was crucial. He was, however, not directive, wisely choosing not to be involved in educational details. He thus remained above the internal debates and dissension, but worked assiduously within broader academic and political environments to ensure acceptance of whatever was ultimately decided. Obviously, that left him in a position of strength whichever way the final decision went.

The widespread engagement of so many members of faculty and the open-ended nature of the committees were crucial for developing ownership, acknowledged to be essential to ensure change. It does, however, make discussion prolonged, repetitive and unpredictable when attendance is erratic. Cross-membership of committees helped communication but imposed a real load on the individuals concerned. The positive spin-offs from the involvement of staff from all over Faculty included the emergence of new cross-disciplinary collaborations and even friendships, not only in teaching but also in research. The Faculty developed a more unified 'feel'. During implementation, even more were drawn into the process, forging even more links.

Effective communication remains a major issue for a widespread faculty like Sydney. The open committees and the workshops run by each of the planning groups ensured participation and involvement. Nevertheless, with so much development in parallel, academic and clinical staff often reported a sense of not quite knowing what was going on. Later, the implementation of a sophisticated intranet to deliver curriculum resources – now the Sydney 'trademark' (http://www.gmp.usyd.edu.au) – revolutionized communication within the Faculty while enhancing student learning.

Although some students in the old programme were bitterly resentful of the time and effort expended by staff in developing the new programme, others became key and enthusiastic contributors. Their continuing support, insights and input were enormously helpful. They selflessly and imaginatively assisted first in planning and later in implementation. The value of such dedicated student input cannot be overestimated, and not only from the material contributions.

The four themes provided a powerful means of integration, not only for planning but also later for assessment, management and review. Consulting the previously unused documents, longitudinal 'vertical stream' groups went on to develop the integrated curriculum. The programme was thus designed to ensure ongoing progressive development across four years. New educational methods were considered: problem-based learning was adopted to meet some of the core values of self-direction, teamwork, student-centeredness, clinical relevance, reasoning and integration. Interestingly, that decision aroused less passion than the goals or issues of discipline-based teaching.

What of traditional departments? The integrated curriculum came at a price and the anguish of the original opponent professor (and others) remains unassuaged. The overlap of teaching two concurrent curricula along with ongoing planning created excessive work. In the short term, the many staff who were totally committed to the new philosophies found it anachronistic to teach students in the old curriculum using discarded practices. Alternatively, others find the new methodologies uncomfortable and feel that their subject-based expertise is undervalued. Careful modelling had previously demonstrated that campus staff teaching loads overall would not increase. In the longer term, though, departmental contributions have inevitably altered, and relative funding now painfully reflects the new balances. Further restructuring of the Faculty into larger groupings is necessarily under way, a threatening prospect to most departments. Unfortunately, these perceived negative effects are amplified by a reduction in overall University funding.

Early in planning, we discovered that two other medical schools – Flinders and Queensland – were independently considering a similar change. Together we formed the Consortium of Graduate Medical Schools, which acted as a mechanism of mutual support and a valuable forum for discussion of admissions, learning, curriculum, assessment and evaluation. It was good not to be alone in all this! Local factors determined that the strategies adopted by each Consortium school were ultimately different, but there was throughout a sense of common purpose and a lively exchange of educational ideas. A collegial approach – unusual between educational institutions – can be thoroughly recommended.

CHAPTER 8

FORWARD FROM THE RETREAT

Case reporter: Peter Schwartz

Issues raised

This case study explores the issue of how to go about developing and promoting a proposal to introduce PBL on a large scale into the pre-clinical curriculum of a long-established, traditional medical school.

Background

The University of Otago Medical School is the older of the two medical schools in New Zealand. It is a public institution and was founded in 1875. It has for many years had a traditional curriculum based on the British system. The course is six years long: the first year is 'pre-medical' for students who have just completed secondary school; the second and third years are the first and second pre-clinical years, respectively; the fourth and fifth years are clinical years; the sixth year is a 'trainee intern' year. Class sizes have been between 150 and 200 students per year in recent years. Teaching staff numbers are around 275–300, supplemented by a large number of clinicians.

PART 1

'All right – if there's no further discussion, could we have a show of hands about the red group's recommendation? All those in favour?... Against?... The "ayes" have it.'

Wow! This looked likely to prove interesting (not to say entertaining!). Participants in the Faculty retreat had just agreed to support a recommendation that PBL be introduced on a large scale to the pre-clinical curriculum. How would the administration handle it? Would Otago soon join the growing ranks of medical schools around the world using PBL?

Such were my thoughts early in 1986, some 15 years after I had arrived at the University of Otago Medical School. I had long been interested in teaching and in improving the medical curriculum, but I felt frustrated by the apparent lack of interest in medical education issues among my colleagues, teachers in other departments, and the administration. Despite a round of curricular revision in the late 1960s, any change had been pretty minimal and there was still plenty of room for improvement. Nothing much happened to the curriculum at Otago during the 1970s and early 1980s.

However, not even so distant a place as New Zealand could avoid being touched by the winds of change from overseas. At the same time as there was a growing disquiet among some faculty members with the state of the curriculum, reports of curricular developments from other countries reached us and were noted. Having a neighbour as near as the University of Newcastle (New South Wales, Australia) adopt PBL in 1978 demonstrated just how close to us these influences were getting. By the time the recommendations in the influential GPEP report (The Panel on the General Professional Education of the Physician and College Preparation for Medicine, 1984) reached us at the end of 1984, we were in the mood to respond.

After two Faculty retreats (in February 1985 and April 1986), there was substantial agreement that the Otago curriculum had several major defects and that they included:

- inadequate skills in self-directed learning among the students and inadequate opportunity in the curriculum for the students to develop such skills;
- declining levels of enjoyment of and enthusiasm for the medical curriculum among students as they progressed through it;
- low levels of satisfaction among teaching staff;
- overload of the curriculum with detailed factual content;
- an excess of didactic teaching that did not meet the needs of students with varying abilities or learning styles;
- lack of any clear statement of overall purpose, goals, or objectives for the undergraduate programme; and
- failure of the curriculum to prepare students to meet the expectations of the public with respect to attitudes and communication skills.

To me and some of the others who had long been interested in the curriculum, this list was not surprising. The defects were neither new nor confined to Otago Medical School. What *was* surprising was that teaching staff attending the second retreat were recommending the introduction of PBL (by 1988, no less!) as the way to solve our curricular problems. We had virtually no one at Otago with any experience of PBL and few people who knew much about it. We had Deans who were supportive of but not enthusiasts for major curricular change. And we had a large, old medical school with a long history of a traditional curriculum, a teaching staff and student body that mostly had traditional backgrounds in and attitudes to education – and a lot of sceptics among the large number of faculty members who had not attended the retreat. It was no wonder, then, that I thought the future could be both interesting and entertaining after this retreat. How would the Dean of Faculty respond?

If you were the Dean of Faculty and responsible for acting on the recommendation of the 1986 retreat to implement PBL in the pre-clinical curriculum (possibly within two years), how would you go about it? What steps would you take?
Given the details about Otago Medical School, the people, and the circumstances surrounding the recommendation to introduce PBL, how do you think the administration actually responded? What actions were taken? What do you think the outcome was?

PART 2

The one advantage we did have at the time of the recommendation from the 1986 retreat was that we already had in place a group that could oversee the preparation of any plan for implementation of PBL. This was the Faculty Curriculum Committee, the group that had organized the two retreats. The Dean of Faculty asked this group to act on the recommendation. Chaired by a dedicated, methodical academic, the Committee promptly developed a plan to investigate the feasibility of introducing PBL to the Otago pre-clinical curriculum. At the heart of the investigation was a series of working parties. The Problems Working Party was responsible for designing the plan for the small-group PBL in the new curriculum and for considering methods for assessing student performance. The Objectives Working Party was given the task of defining appropriate objectives for the medical curriculum. The Early Clinical Contact Working Party was asked to design a programme of early clinical contact that could form the initial phase of the ongoing clinical component of the new curriculum. Each working party was to prepare detailed proposals for consideration by the Faculty. Waiting to supplement these groups were a Learning Materials Working Party (to design appropriate learning materials for PBL), a Specialist Credits Working Party (to investigate the place of elective work in the new curriculum), and a Resources Subcommittee (comprising Deans and those responsible for considering resource issues associated with the proposal). Finally, a small Medical Education Development Unit was established, in the first instance to support the feasibility study. It consisted of two senior academic staff with interests in medical education (each on a half-time basis), a part-time secretary, and a full-time Research Fellow.

All of these groups were identified within a few months of the 1986 retreat and most started working promptly. At the time, I was a member of the Faculty Curriculum Committee and I was soon part of both the Problems and Objectives Working Parties. It was an intensely busy but also extremely stimulating interval. With reasonably small memberships of dedicated workers, a committed overseer (the chair of the Faculty Curriculum Committee), and good liaison and support through the Medical Education Development Unit, the groups made excellent progress with their tasks. Concurrently, several small-scale trials of PBL were organized to demonstrate the process to teaching staff and students and to provide them with at least a minimum of experience with the method.

For me, it was by far the most satisfying interval I had had at Otago up to that point. It would be pleasing to say that it was also ultimately successful. Sadly, that was not the case. Although the various groups involved in the investigation regularly consulted with and sought input from others who were not members of the working parties, and despite attempts to keep the Faculty informed of developments and 'on side', discontent and resistance were growing. Many people felt left out of the deliberations and felt threatened by the ideas that were being developed. Up to this point they were a 'silent majority', but when they realized that the proposal was not simply going to go away on its own, they mounted a stiff resistance.

Among others, concerns were expressed about the prospect of loss of emphasis on the basic medical sciences, inadequate coverage of important topics, loss of departmental control over course content and assessment, inability of the students to cope with the new system, the possible use of detailed objectives to force a radical change to the curriculum, diversion of students' attention from the study of basic medical sciences by early clinical contact, inability of the students to deal with early clinical contact because of immaturity and lack of knowledge, and so on and so on. The list of criticisms was formidable, though hardly novel. Most disheartening were some of the general statements that were submitted along with (or even in place of) the input that was requested from departments by the Problems Working Party.

> But what I feel really must be said is that this document demonstrates very clearly that the whole exercise could never be seen to be an adequate alternative to systematic teaching… I do hope that we could use this juncture to convey the deep misgivings of the faculty as a whole about whither we are being manoeuvred. (From a teacher in a pre-clinical department.)

> We are *unanimous* in our view that the second year course in _____ *must* retain a strong basis of formal instruction by staff who are specialists in the subject. We are very concerned that your Working Party is putting a great deal of effort into planning a course that we know *now* will be unacceptable not only to us but to

the majority of our colleagues in other pre-clinical disciplines and that this effort is simply wasting time that could be spent with great profit in developing a revised course that will be universally accepted. (From the chairman of another pre-clinical department.)

The last straw was added when some of the departments that taught in the first pre-clinical year decided to pre-empt any large-scale imposed change by modifying their courses within their own disciplines to incorporate some of the principles of PBL. Although far from true PBL, these innovations tended to be described as such by their originators and were used as yet another argument against the introduction of PBL on a large scale: 'We're already doing it successfully ourselves!'

These developments demonstrated how little support there actually was for the introduction of PBL at Otago. Without the issue ever being brought to Faculty for a formal vote, the proposal was abandoned early in 1988. The Faculty Curriculum Committee merely expressed the hope that the departmental initiatives and some of the ideas generated during the investigation might be built upon for further progress in developing the curriculum. We were left with a detailed list of problems for the early phase of a PBL course and a well developed proposal for early clinical contact (neither of which was now wanted by anyone), sets of general and intermediate objectives for the medical curriculum (which were deemed to be useful enough on their own that they were eventually adopted by the Faculty), a series of piecemeal changes to individual courses incorporating some of the principles of PBL – and a defunct Medical Education Development Unit (from which funding was withdrawn when the unit appeared not to be delivering value for money, notwithstanding its original mandate to devote itself to the PBL proposal). In that list of 'achievements' were a few positives, but it is arguable whether the results were commensurate with the time, effort and frustration involved.

The outcome at Otago was considerably less than had been hoped for. What do you think went wrong? What factors led to the disappointing result? How might things have been done differently?

CASE REPORTER'S DISCUSSION

The method that was chosen to promote the introduction of PBL at Otago clearly didn't work. Whether any method would have been successful is moot, but there were certainly several factors that militated against success in the method we chose. As part of our effort to learn (and to let others learn) from the episode, we wrote a book describing our experiences (Schwartz *et al*, 1994). In it, we reflected on our achievements (such as they were) and on the factors that probably contributed to the ultimate failure of the proposal to introduce PBL. Had we recognized the importance of these factors *before* embarking on our investigation, perhaps things would have turned out differently. Others contemplating similar changes would be well advised to be aware of them.

From our perspective, the major factors were as follows:

- We did not sufficiently recognize the extreme difficulty of making such a large change in a long-established medical school.
- We grossly overestimated the degree of enthusiasm among staff for the proposed change. Those attending the second retreat were definitely enthusiastic, but they represented only a small proportion of the total teaching staff.
- We gave inadequate attention to many of the known obstacles to change in the medical curriculum. Some of the most important at Otago were:
  - fears about loss of control over the curriculum by departments and about threats to the independence of individual disciplines within the course;
  - a fear of loss of control over assessment of students and a worry about the adequacy of assessment in the proposed course;
  - comfort with the *status quo*, especially in contrast to the unknown or only partially understood system that was being proposed;
  - reluctance of faculty to accept changes to teaching styles, especially when the new styles would demand new skills that would require time and effort to develop;
  - a reward structure typical of many universities, which emphasized research and clinical service for promotion (and even for study leave), so that there was little incentive to devote time to educational matters or to the development of new skills in teaching;
  - a resistance to any major change that gives the appearance of being forced upon unwilling participants too quickly;
  - a perceived lack of adequate resources for the preparation and implementation of such a labour-intensive programme; and
  - a lack of conviction among many teachers that the proposed teaching methods would work or that they would be better than the old ones, or even that anything was wrong with the old system.
- We had not developed an effective strategy to overcome the various obstacles. Others have identified the components of such a strategy, and we can add some from our own experiences. Some of the most important from Otago's perspective would have been to:
  - build a broad base of 'ownership' among those who will be expected to implement the proposed change, by involving a much higher proportion of teaching staff at all stages of preparation of the new programme;

- ensure adequate dissemination of information about the proposed change to all who would be affected by it, once again by involving more staff in preparing the programme and by frequent newsletters and meetings;
- ensure that the proposed change is perceived as valuable and challenging, by emphasizing the likely benefits of the new programme to students, teachers and the school;
- enlist key people to provide appropriate leadership and authority (especially Deans and teams of faculty well versed in educational issues) and recruit (or at least neutralize) important people who are conservatives;
- allow sufficient time to overcome resistance, postponing or accelerating events depending on conditions;
- provide opportunities for faculty to acquire necessary new knowledge and skills for the innovative programme;
- increase rewards for educational scholarship and teaching so that teaching staff will have an incentive to devote time to designing and participating in the new programme; and
- develop understanding and enthusiasm for the innovative course by having teachers participate.

Although some parts of such a strategy were employed at Otago, some crucial elements were lacking. In particular, no one at the highest levels of the administration exhibited the very high degree of commitment needed to persuade faculty members to accept the proposal. Indeed, Abrahamson (1998) maintains that such a person is essential to the successful introduction of PBL.

- At the time when the proposal was being considered, very little of the pressure for change was coming from outside the medical school. Some sources suggest that such external pressure is an important factor in promoting the acceptance of a change as profound as that of adopting PBL on a large scale.
- By the time a decision was required on whether or not to implement PBL, most departments that taught in the pre-clinical course had introduced their own innovative courses. This effectively helped to pre-empt any move to impose across-the-board PBL.

Finally, reviewers of our book reminded us of the importance of managing both the process of change and the people involved in it, and the importance of local ownership of the change. They also suggested that it would have been wise to actually have instituted change rather than merely to have prepared in detail for it. For example, an actual pilot programme could have followed on from the small-scale trials of PBL, to show faculty what could be achieved – even as we continued to polish lists of goals, objectives and cases/problems.

Since that abortive attempt to introduce PBL at Otago we have, in fact, implemented a new pre-clinical curriculum (starting in 1997) (Schwartz *et al*, 1999). Although much less ambitious than that embodied in the earlier proposal, the new curriculum incorporates some of its key features, including an increase in small-group, case-based teaching, much of it interdisciplinary; a programme of early clinical contact; and a course that deals with professional attitudes and skills. Although this might have been expected to generate the same resistance as before, this has not happened, perhaps partly because the ideas did not appear so revolutionary and partly because:

> a different strategy and set of tactics from those used in the previous round of curricular revision were adopted. An Associate Dean for pre-clinical education was appointed to guide the new curriculum into existence; no such leader had been present before. A large 'implementation and development committee', with wide representation, had the task of generating the new curriculum and seeing that a series of course or module convenors carried out the detailed preparations; in the previous round, small groups, mostly invisible to the majority of faculty, had done the detailed planning and had then presented startling proposals, apparently without much consultation. A 'get in there and do it' mentality was fostered by affirming that the new curriculum would have to be ready for implementation in 1996 (subsequently postponed to 1997 when the original date was found to be just too optimistic); in the earlier round, the various working groups were expected to present completed proposals for discussion and decision, unwisely delaying any real action and allowing opposition to the proposals to grow. (Schwartz *et al*, 1999)

In other words, we applied some of the important lessons learnt from our earlier failure. I think it unlikely that Otago will move to a fully PBL curriculum, but the successful introduction of the new curriculum has made staff and students more comfortable with the notion of curricular change. Perhaps early application of our lessons by others will pave the way for successful implementation of PBL – at the very least, awareness of the lessons may prevent a lot of heartache and frustration.

References

Abrahamson, S (1998) 'Obstacles to establishing problem-based learning', *Journal of Dental Education*, **62**, pp 656–59

The Panel on the General Professional Education of the Physician and College Preparation for Medicine (1984) *Physicians for the Twenty-first Century. The GPEP Report*, Association of American Medical Colleges, Washington, DC

Schwartz, P L, Heath, C J and Egan, A G (1994) *The Art of the Possible. Ideas from a traditional medical school engaged in curricular revision*, University of Otago Press, Dunedin, New Zealand

Schwartz, P L, Loten, E G and Miller, A P (1999) 'Curriculum reform at the University of Otago Medical School', *Academic Medicine*, **74**, pp 675–79

ISSUES RELATING TO TEACHERS

CHAPTER 9

Too little, too late?

Case reporter: Carol-Ann Courneya

Issues raised

This case study addresses the importance of group- and self-evaluation and timely feedback in the tutorial process and how it can be compromised by an over-zealous desire to include too much content.

Background

In 1997, an interdepartmental, skills-based graduate course was offered for the first time within the Faculty of Medicine at The University of British Columbia (UBC). The students were biomedical graduate students enrolled in their first year of a Masters programme. Using a PBL approach, the course addressed skills important to such students: identifying testable hypotheses, articulating scientific concepts, developing efficient enquiry strategies, matching hypotheses to appropriate experimental designs and developing appropriate ethical and professional behaviours. The cases or 'problems' used in the course described situations that biomedical graduate students might expect to encounter during the course of their own programmes. The first run of this course included six students, a number of guest scientists (each of whom was responsible for a given case) and myself as facilitator. Although the guest scientists came and went with cases, I was present as the principal facilitator throughout the entire semester.

PART 1

It was day one of the inaugural run of the new graduate student skills course and the stakes were high for making it a success. The six students were selected from five distinct basic science departments at UBC (Anatomy, Physiology, Neuroscience, Biochemistry and Medical Genetics).

All the students realized this was a 'novel' course and were interested in it, but they were curious about how it would be different from the standard content-rich graduate courses they were also enrolled in. Right from the beginning this was a unique experience for them because of the small size of the class. The students were all freshly graduated from undergraduate science courses where the smallest classes had been 30–50 people. On that first day, they were invited to tell each other about their educational backgrounds and their interests both in and outside of work. I involved myself in those discussions and told the students how I had come to my interest in education and what I did outside of work hours. Together we developed a number of ground rules that would govern the way we worked as a group, one of them being that we would all be expected to take opportunities to evaluate our contributions to the group dynamics and to receive feedback from the group concerning our evaluations.

As the tutorials unfolded and the students discussed the different problems, a pattern began to emerge. The tutorials were generally lively two-hour discussions surrounding the content of each new case. In the initial tutorials, cursory attempts were made at self- and group-evaluation, but as the group seemed to be working well together, there was never much to say, and as the cases became more complex, even these cursory attempts were largely abandoned.

A complicating factor was that, since all the cases were new, I usually had no idea how long the discussion of any particular case might take. The cases were interdepartmental in nature, as were the students, so at any given time some students were finding the content easy while some were finding it challenging. This meant that the discussions were generally lengthy as there was an agreement within the group that we would proceed only when everyone could understand the content. Thus our regular two-hour tutorials were often filled to capacity with discussions of the content of the case.

About a quarter of the way through the semester, I began to sense that one of the students (Tracey) was dissatisfied with any time spent discussing what she considered to be 'soft' issues (such as professional conduct, scientific ethics or lab safety). Tracey had, in the beginning, been a vociferous and innovative contributor to all discussions. I had valued her contributions and felt that her enthusiasm had been a great benefit to the group. Lately, she had begun to arrive late and contributed minimally to the discussions. In one 'case', the students were asked to role-play through a series of critical incidents demonstrating interpersonal and ethical dilemmas they might encounter with peers or supervisors in their labs. The now reticent Tracey obviously considered these role-plays a joke (once even saying: 'These role-plays are ridiculous. Let's get back to the substance of our learning issues.') She clearly did not take them at all seriously, an attitude that diminished the effect they had on the entire group. Although I acknowledged that a problem had developed, I was already sensitized to the impatience I perceived when the group had to deal with 'non-science' process issues.

Another student whose participation concerned me was a foreign student named Fazir. His participation decreased after a tutorial in which he had urged the group to include a particular question in an ethics form they were constructing. The group disagreed, and his attempt to explain his rationale (which admittedly was a bit hard to follow) was discounted and his question was discarded. Since that time, although he seemed to be listening critically throughout the tutorials, his contributions were infrequent.

I hoped that if we carried on we could deal with these issues during a tutorial that I was going to devote entirely to evaluation and feedback and that was coming up in two weeks (half-way through the semester). Surely, I thought, any issues or dissatisfactions could be ironed out at that time.

The day for the self- and group-evaluation arrived. I had gone over my notes from the previous tutorials and prepared some specific feedback (their strengths and weaknesses) for each of the students. As well, I was prepared to evaluate my own role as the tutorial leader. I began the discussion by modelling a frank self-evaluation where I talked about my strengths as a facilitator and what I felt I needed to improve on. As one might expect from students who had no training in feedback, they merely agreed with what I said were my strengths and did not comment on what I said I needed to improve on.

Then I asked each of them to evaluate his or her own individual contributions to the group, after which the rest of the group could give feedback on the evaluation. Each student made cursory statements about her or his contributions, eg 'I think I contribute too frequently' or 'I need to speak up more' – pretty standard issues. In response, the other students were generally complimentary, saying things like, 'I don't think you talk too much' or 'I think you always have something valuable to contribute.' The entire exercise took about 15 minutes. I prompted the group with questions like: 'Is there anything about the dynamic of this group that is interfering with your ability to learn and participate freely?' and 'Is there anything the group (or you) could do to improve the learning environment?' Nothing much came from these questions. I was about to close everything down when, suddenly, Tracey, the student who lately had become a non-contributor, spoke up and said, 'I don't think people are being very honest. Personally, I think this course has become a total waste of time and I no longer even prepare for the tutorials any more. I'm not the only one slacking off and you,' she said pointing at me, 'don't do anything about it. There are no consequences for not doing our work.' She continued, 'I thought this would be an interesting course where we would learn about molecular biology, but we have spent way too much time dealing with soft issues and I have learnt next to nothing about real science.'

What do you think has contributed to this sudden outburst?
Is the situation salvageable?

If you were the person faced with this situation, what would you do next?
What do you think the actual outcome was?

PART 2

Following the outburst, there was a stunned silence, after which I asked the group, 'Do the rest of you feel the same way?' Other students in the group began to vigorously defend their past contributions and say that they had worked very hard to prepare for the cases. In particular, Litia, a student who had little background in cell biology, said she found most of the cases very challenging. Other students said that although they liked the cases that centred on 'science', they valued the discussions on ethical and professional dilemmas, and that was what set this course apart from other 'standard' graduate courses. On the other hand, other students agreed with the initial comments that there had been little in the way of constructive feedback by me to guide them as to the level of their contributions. I listened carefully to all the comments and started by thanking them all for their candour. I acknowledged that providing more constructive verbal feedback on the quality of individual contributions would have been desirable and said that I would make stronger attempts to do that for the rest of the semester. I told Tracey that I had indeed noticed the reduction in the quality of her contributions and had erred in not giving her timely feedback on my observations.

As if a door had been opened to honesty, Fazir spoke up and said that he had felt shut down by the group during the discussion about the ethics form, and he felt his difficulty with language prevented him from explaining his rationale. He said, 'If you would have given me time I could have explained myself better, but you speak so quickly that I feel I have to say everything fast and so I get confused with my English.' The other students in the group looked taken aback and one student, Glen, asked Fazir what the group could do to make him feel part of the discussions. Fazir said that from time to time he'd like the group to ask for his opinion and then give him time to phrase it carefully. The students agreed to do this. After a pregnant pause, Litia said, almost apologetically, 'I know, Tracey, that you think that we aren't working hard, but I am having to learn the molecular biology from square one and I'm finding it very difficult. I think you felt my presentations were pretty basic, but that is the best I can do at this point'. Tracey immediately replied, 'No, I actually thought your presentation was really good; you presented the "big picture" without getting lost in the details.' Kathy, who was a biochemistry graduate student, then said, 'Litia, if you are having trouble with the cell biology, why don't you let me help you? I've been learning it for six years now.' The discussion seemed to clear the air for everyone.

The next day I received a long e-mail from Tracey, the student who had criticized the course, saying that on reflection she had learnt a lot more in the course (science and otherwise) than she had given it credit for. She had been surprised to hear that other students had been working hard and that indeed they valued the opportunity to explore the 'non-science' issues. She said that after the feedback session her commitment to the course had been revitalized and she was looking forward to the rest of the semester. In fact, there were changes for all of us during the remainder of the semester. We carved out time on a more regular basis for self- and group-evaluation. This was often difficult since the cases continued to be new and untested, and from time to time they filled our two-hour blocks of tutorial time. The difference was that the students, who had begun to see the value in evaluation and feedback, would stay on after the sessions in order to make sure we accomplished it on a regular basis. As a result, Tracey returned to her role as enthusiastic contributor and even handled the good-natured ribbing from the group when we dealt with 'soft' issues. Fazir actually took the time during a subsequent tutorial to explain his rationale for wanting to include the ethics question, and it turned out it was linked to a cultural issue from his country. Once fully explained, it had quite an impact on the group. Over the rest of the semester, Kathy and Litia met from time to time and had informal cell biology tutorials. As for me, I paid more attention to the quality of their contributions during tutorials and gave them feedback right away as to what was good and what needed further improvement.

What are the significant issues from this case for your own teaching?
How do you balance the demands of content and process in curricular
programmes such as PBL that feature teaching in small groups?
What are the implications for faculty development?

CASE REPORTER'S DISCUSSION

This experience precipitated several changes in the nature of the cases for the following year's course. Knowing how complex some of the students found the cases (especially the cases outside of their particular sub-specialty), I simplified them (or extended them over several tutorials) so that they could be realistically accomplished and still allow for regular self- and group-evaluation. I also made it abundantly clear to students who were thinking of enrolling in the course that this was not designed as a course whose primary goal was to teach 'cell biology'. Instead it was a course that would provide them with practice in developing a variety of skills that would prepare them for life after graduate school. To some extent this was made easier by the fact that there were now students who had taken the course and who reinforced for potential students that the skills they had practised were indeed important and useful. In fact, almost all the students who enrolled in the second year did so because of positive comments made by senior graduate students. Lastly, I made it a priority to give students timely, regular feedback regarding their written and oral contributions to the tutorials.

The experience taught me two important lessons about running a tutorial-based skills course. The first is that there must be a balance between curriculum content and time built in for regular self- and group-evaluation. This might seem elementary to some readers – 'of course you shouldn't overload content at the expense of process' – however, in my zeal to create a new course that would interest and challenge the students I forgot how easy it is to unbalance the equilibrium between process and content. This is influenced by the fact that students who are new to self- and group-evaluation are often uncomfortable with it in the beginning and it is easy to mistake this discomfort as impatience with the process. To be effective, self-/group-evaluation and feedback must take place in a setting that is psychologically safe (Carroll and Goldberg, 1989). Establishing that environment takes time, a commodity that may be in short supply in a curriculum that has been overloaded by content.

It is easy to forget that every group grows through a number of developmental stages (Tuckman, 1965). During the initial stage the group members are polite, and they seem on the surface quite harmonious. There is indeed little to say to criticize group dynamics during this time. Thus it is easier to abandon time dedicated to evaluation and to justify this by saying that the group works well – the assumption being that self-evaluation and feedback are useful only when something is wrong and in need of fixing. In reality, positive behaviours can be rewarded during early tutorials as a way of encouraging norms of behaviour and establishing a safe environment for candid and useful reflection later when conflicts arise. In addition, the tutor can make use of this time to model positive, reflective self-evaluation. Having said that, it requires that the tutor have adequate training and practice in self- and group-evaluation. This has implications for faculty development. In order to model quality self-evaluation, the facilitators need training in how to do it themselves as well as practice at discerning when there are problems with group dynamics. This is not standard training for most basic scientists, although with more and more medical faculties embracing PBL, this is starting to change. Standard tutor training, however, is often limited to basic tutoring skills and little time is spent in training the facilitators to manage group dynamics and to perform self- and group-evaluation.

The second lesson I learnt was the importance of giving regular, timely feedback to the students. Standards for the quality of work (written and oral) must be established early in a new course and then maintained throughout the semester. Giving quality oral feedback is a skill that requires practice by the tutor. It is much easier to tell a student that his or her work is excellent than to illustrate the flaws in someone's presentation or paper and to help the student find ways to improve it. A sense of trust must be developed whereby students understand that you have their best academic interests at heart.

Strategies for giving quality feedback have been well established (Brinko, 1993; Davies and Jacobs, 1985), and these allow students to see what their strengths are and also where there is room for improvement. As with self- and group-evaluation, providing feedback to students takes time and thus must be allowed for in a regular component of tutorial time. This requires re-shaping the equilibrium between content and process.

Finally, the case illustrates well some implications of the facilitator's role. Heron (1999) has identified six dimensions of facilitation: planning, meaning, confronting, feeling, structuring and valuing. The case is a good example of differences emerging within a group regarding (especially) the planning, confronting, feeling and valuing dimensions, and it demonstrates the usefulness of self- and group-evaluation in resolving them.

References

Brinko, K (1993) 'The practice of giving feedback to improve teaching: what is effective?', *Journal of Higher Education*, **64**, pp 574–95

Carroll, J G and Goldberg, S R (1989) 'Teaching consultants: a collegial approach to better teaching', *College Teaching*, **37**, pp 143–46

Davies, D and Jacobs, A (1985) '"Sandwiching" complex interpersonal feedback', *Small Group Behaviors*, **16**, pp 387–96

Heron, J (1999) *The Complete Facilitator's Handbook*, Kogan Page, London

Tuckman, B W (1965) 'Developmental sequence in small groups', *Psychological Bulletin*, **63**, pp 384–99

CHAPTER 10

NOT MORE PBL

Case reporter: Elizabeth Farmer

Issues raised

This case study looks at how clinical students' boredom with paper-based PBL can provide a significant challenge to staff who are attempting to maintain PBL in the clinical years of a medical curriculum.

Background

Located in the southern suburbs of the city of Adelaide, the School of Medicine at Flinders University is the second medical school in the State of South Australia. The first class was admitted in 1974 and the current intake comprises about 80 students per year. The School is co-located with a major teaching hospital at the Flinders Medical Centre, enabling easy communication between hospital and University staff. A problem-based, four-year graduate entry medical programme (GEMP) was adopted in 1996.

PART 1

In designing our new programme, we chose PBL cases as the main educational approach for the first two years. Teaching of clinical skills was integrated into these years but took a lesser role. In planning, we visualized the third year as an intensive year of required clinical specialties, ending with a final Objective Structured Clinical Examination (OSCE) and written tests. The fourth year would allow students a wide choice of disciplines to study in various locations, and it would finish with elective programmes. No end-of-year examinations were envisaged for the fourth year, as assessment was to be conducted entirely 'in-course' during and by the various components.

Early on in the curriculum design process, we promoted PBL as an important learning method for the clinical years of the course and not just for the first two years. We cited such arguments as coherence of the educational process throughout the course and the flexibility of PBL in providing appropriate challenges to students at all levels. The Curriculum Committee was convinced and the principle was adopted.

Inevitably, in the early stages of development, we focused our case design efforts on the first two years of the course, where PBL was to be the central educational approach. Little time was available to consider PBL for the clinical years (years three and four) until 1997, the year before the year three programme was to run for the first time. Nevertheless, those of us who were responsible for the General Practice component of third year felt confident that we could come up with the goods. We were all experienced PBL tutors who had been intimately involved in the new curriculum in various capacities since it began. Besides, we had chosen dermatology and longitudinal care as the focus of our first clinical PBL case. These topics had been 'sure fire' winners in the previous course and were always well evaluated. They were important integrating subjects and were common problems.

We found virtually no guidance available in the published literature to help us in our preparations, but a visitor from the University of Kentucky showed us examples of clinical PBL cases that they regarded as successful. These cases had a strong focus on investigation and management and they were conducted in a typical PBL tutorial group. Thinking carefully about the level and sophistication of our students and their need to concentrate on management issues rather than basic sciences during the clinical years, we wrote a management-focused three-part case with dermatology pictures and other clinical documentation provided to enhance realism. The case was well written in the usual style of cases for the first two years.

Our new PBL case was delivered for the first time in 1998, about mid-way through the year, to 30 students in small groups of eight with experienced and enthusiastic PBL tutors, all of whom were general (family) practitioners.

Imagine our dismay when students seemed bored, lacked motivation in the groups and skimmed unenthusiastically over the case. This came as a total surprise, because in our extensive feedback from years one and two the students never mentioned being bored with the typical PBL case approach. The students' evaluations of clinical PBL, both on paper and in focus groups, confirmed our impressions and shed some light on the causes of the problem. On the one hand were comments like:

> We are bored with PBL cases.
> Thank you for your effort, but we are really sick of it (PBL).
> I'm exhausted already, too tired to study.

And on the other hand:

How is this going to help me pass my OSCE?
We need more patient contact… not more paper.
I'm worried about my clinical skills – not my knowledge.

How could we respond to this wholly unanticipated situation?

What might explain the students' reactions?
What could the staff have done to better anticipate these reactions?
Faced with this dilemma, how should the staff now react? Why?

PART 2

We began by trying to get some more insight into the students' perceptions. We held a lengthy discussion with our group. With the help of pizza and other enticements, we learnt that the main issue was the pressure the students felt to be 'up to final examination standard' by the end of the year. Learning clinical skills seemed to be a dominant concern and students were feeling panicky about their progress. They had not yet had the formative clinical test that was scheduled for early the following month.

In addition, our students were obviously tired. Their year had begun early and was intensive. They were doing long hours on the wards for the first time, especially as they had just been doing obstetrics. They really wanted a holiday, but as general practice was the last discipline of the semester, they were still two weeks away from that. Some had already started to 'switch off'.

PBL had lost its shine for many students, who expected clinical PBL to be 'somehow different'. The students expressed boredom with the 'same old' paper case approach, but they had few ideas about how we might achieve an improvement. None the less, they asked us to innovate and 'produce something that will help us in our OSCE as well'. Accepting that the students were rejecting the usual PBL approach, we returned to the drawing board and gathered for a brainstorming session.

First we looked at the big picture. We decided to ask the Curriculum Committee whether the general practice component of year three could be placed earlier in the semester so that the students were not so exhausted when we worked with them. Finding some support from concerned Women's and Children's Health teachers, we also lobbied for the semester to be shortened by a week so that students could have a mid-semester break. We emerged as the first group to teach in the year, when students were fresh from long holidays.

Drawing on our strengths in the use of Standardized Patients (SPs) in teaching, we decided to try a completely new approach to clinical PBL: we would integrate encounters with SPs into a clinical PBL case. We wanted to make use of the realism of the SP encounter to 'bring the case to life' and to provide a realistic clinical skills challenge to the students during the PBL process. As part of this effort, we trained a young woman to portray 'Valerie Pahuja', a mother of one with early cancer of the breast.

We wrote a new three-tutorial clinical case about 'Valerie's' progress from diagnosis to long-term follow-up. The tutorial is structured in two distinct phases. In the first phase, students explore the case for about one hour in a typical PBL format with small group and tutor. They then formulate learning objectives relating to such issues as the pathophysiology of breast masses, clinical findings in breast masses and investigations. After self-directed learning time, the tutorial enters a second phase where the small group then sees the 'patient' in real life. One student is selected to conduct the interview with her, during which the student has to break the news of her unexpected result of cancer. This part of the PBL is integrated with a clinical skills session where students see other SPs who present challenging problems requiring the application of communication skills. Suddenly what was a 'paper case' becomes real and the challenge is evident. The tutor's role has now become that of facilitator of learning in communication skills. Clinical knowledge acquired from study of the objectives has been placed firmly in the immediate context of the clinical skills required to work with a distressed young woman.

The same process is used for the remaining two tutorials as 'Valerie' is followed through alternative therapy and surgery, and finally to a morbid fear of secondary spread. Each time, 'Valerie' returns after the case has developed further on paper. As part of their self-directed learning on the clinical skills issues raised by the case and by their experience during the SP encounter, students are encouraged to use their own patients, other clinician teachers and allied health professionals as resources.

So what was the outcome this time? Thankfully, the students responded very positively to this new format. Typical comments were:

> Loads better than the surgery breast cancer case.
> (The case was valuable in) both medical knowledge and counselling skills.
> (The case) aided my learning – matched theory and clinical skills.
> Fantastic to have the SPs to practise all the consulting skills.
> Made it relevant.
> (The case) has given me concrete skills in dealing with real-life issues.

When we asked whether the case had helped as preparation for the OSCE, we received a resounding 'Yes!' However, perhaps the most honest response was from the student who wrote: 'I hope so!'

What other options might there be for modifying PBL to suit students in the clinical years of a professional course like medicine?

CASE REPORTER'S DISCUSSION

The difficulties we experienced with our first approach related to three factors associated with students' entry into the 'clinical' portion of the curriculum: a change in students' attitudes, a major change in the prevailing culture of teaching and, if anything, a heightening of the ever-present fear of assessment. In terms of attitudes, we discovered that students' views of the value of PBL in the third year were not as we had expected. We assumed that the major difference required between PBL cases in the first two years and in our new 'clinical PBL' case would be in content: success would be ensured by having a case that was clinically focused, with a diagnostic and management orientation. However, to our chagrin, we discovered that content was not enough. We needed to introduce a process that was more sophisticated and relevant as well.

In terms of culture, the students were essentially saying, 'We are nearly doctors now!' They saw PBL as a pre-clinical mode, which they felt had been superseded by the more enticing and satisfying clinical 'hands on' experience of real patients. They were bored with the contrived paper patients. It became obvious to us that students perceived a dichotomy between the first two 'pre-clinical' years and the second two 'clinical' years. This occurred despite our awareness of the potential existence of such a problem and our attempts to create an integrated whole-curriculum approach by using graded clinical contact throughout the course.

Anecdotally, it appeared that many of our clinician teachers, most of whom had little or no experience of PBL, were not integrating their ward-based teaching with any other teaching approach. Therefore, the intention of exploiting the value of PBL in clinical training, or seeking to use it to enhance patient-based learning, was under threat from both students and their clinician teachers.

Fear of assessment remained, as ever, a driving force behind student response. With six months to go until the OCSE and nine hours of written tests, students wanted to see clear prospects of their learning experiences helping them in their examination performance. In contrast to the non-graded assessment in the first two years, year three was graded, and this added further pressure.

After our first attempt, consultation with our students about how to proceed was an important next step. We tried to build a problem-solving partnership with our students. Although the causes of the problems had become apparent, the students could contribute few ideas about how to solve them. None the less, the student-staff relationship built up through years of PBL was valuable in the dialogue.

The enthusiasm and skills of our team and their innovative thinking, coupled with a genuine responsiveness to student feedback, enabled us to create a successful alternative. We will never know, however, whether we might have prevented this situation from arising by, for example, using some of the focus group times during years one and two to obtain prospective comments from the students to warn us that they sought a change from typical PBL for the clinical course.

CHAPTER 11

Why do they ignore it?

Case reporters: Marlene Lindberg and Gordon Greene

Issues raised

This case deals with the problem of getting students in a PBL medical school curriculum to pay attention to important learning issues that do not appear to them to be central to the patient cases being studied – in this example, the behavioural and social components of illness.

Background

The events described took place at the University of Hawaii's John A Burns School of Medicine. There are between 55 and 65 students in each class at this medical school, located in Honolulu. The observations and conversations in the case took place in the autumn of 1999, 10 years after implementation of PBL in the two pre-clinical years of the curriculum.

PART 1

'Marlene, have you got a bit of time to talk? Yes, this is Gordon. You said I could call to talk over this new group of first-year students I'm working with in a Unit 1 PBL tutorial. We had a great session on Thursday. I want to tell you about that – but it was also such a painful contrast to my Unit 3 students last spring that I'd like your help in sorting out some thoughts. It's the same struggle we've talked about many times – we say that the behavioural perspective on health and illness is important for students to develop during their first two years – and they start out respecting that – but then how quickly it fades. I've got a great group of Unit 1 students for whom this perspective is still important and I'd like your advice on how to continue to strengthen it with them.'

Gordon and Marlene are colleagues in the Office of Medical Education. Gordon, an experienced PBL tutor and trainer of new faculty tutors, and Marlene, coordinator of programme evaluation and educational research, had worked together on curriculum issues for many years. Both support the way that medical students at the University of Hawaii are instructed to consider four broad perspectives (biological, clinical, behavioural and population) as they work through the 83 patient cases that form the foundation of the pre-clinical curriculum. Both are also acutely aware of the difficulty of sustaining a focus on behavioural issues in the PBL cases in spite of the exposure students have to simulated and real patients from the time they enter medical school.

Gordon continued on the phone: 'So here was my Unit 1 group, students who have been here only one month, and we were tackling the Charles Browning case. Remember, he's the 62-year-old part-Hawaiian man who arrives at the emergency room with a complaint of chest pain. The students and I had already gone through two tutorial sessions to discuss Mr Browning and his subsequent diagnosis of a heart attack. Their take-home "learning issues" included the usual list of topics related to heart attacks: anatomy, physiology, emergency care systems in the community, and so on.

'Last Monday we had our third discussion of the case and the students were proposing additional learning issues related to "the risks and benefits of thrombolytic therapy" and "the pharmacological mechanism of nitro-glycerin". I didn't like the way things were headed so I asked, "Are you guys getting much out of this?" I felt hesitant about challenging the group, but I decided to go ahead and let them know what was on my mind. "How much do you care about these things at this point in the case? This is the last day we'll be proposing learning issues for Mr Browning. Are the learning issues you've listed so far today really the things you most want to know about this patient? You seem bored, like you're just going through the motions."

'Keiko quickly spoke up, "You know, my Dad went through this and his doctor talked all about exercise and diet, but my Dad wouldn't listen. He's hardheaded. If it weren't for my Mom..." and the group began to discuss how people who've had heart attacks actually behave. After 10 minutes, I again challenged the group to describe what they would most like to learn about and present at their follow-up meeting three days hence. They came up with two good biological issues, but what really got me excited were the other three learning issues, issues that showed me the students really wanted to understand some things about human behaviour, both that of the patient and that of the physician in this case.

'Keiko asked the first question, "What is the physician's role in changing harmful behaviour in a patient?" After a moment's thought, she recognized that what she really wanted to know was, "How does a physician personally cope with patients who refuse to listen to advice that could save their lives?"

Alan was obviously struck by Keiko's earlier comment about the role of her mother in her father's recovery and decided to investigate the role of the family in helping a patient recover from a heart attack. Joan wanted to know more about the components of a cardiac rehabilitation programme but, like Keiko, she realized this didn't cut to the heart of her question. She really wanted to know, "What power does a physician have in determining the outcome of a patient's cardiac rehabilitation?"

'These were heart-felt questions and the students went after them with a passion. As impressive as the questions were, the answers they brought back to the group on Thursday were even more impressive. Keiko's discussion of physicians' coping mechanisms was based on interviews with a primary care physician and two cardiologists, in which she asked them the question she had posed to the group. Alan had edited a story about a man's recovery from a heart attack into a script for role-play by the group. Joan had read Howard Brody's wonderful text, *The Healer's Power*, and challenged the group with her hypothesis that a physician's most significant role following a patient's heart attack is to foster emotional recovery.

'It was great! I wish you could have seen it. The discussion they generated was as rich as it gets, but what especially pleased me was that they had done such thorough investigations into the realm of patient and physician behaviour. But – you knew this was coming – why can't they sustain this ability and interest much beyond the first few months of medical school? I'm thinking of the Unit 3 group I tutored a few months ago near the end of their first year.

'The case was an evocative description of a 55-year-old woman's encounter with colon cancer. The woman, Mrs Haneda, lived in Japan and was visiting her daughter in Hawaii when she had a sudden attack of vomiting and abdominal pain. Even though she subsequently had surgery for removal of a cancerous section of her colon and an ileostomy, her daughter and husband were adamant that she not be told the diagnosis because such disclosure would be "devastating". It was stated in the case that, although disclosure of cancer has become more common in Japan despite a strong cultural taboo, physicians in Japan respect family opinion when there is strong consensus that the patient should not be told. The problem faced by the physician in the case was that a sensitive inquiry of the patient about her expectations regarding her care in Hawaii revealed that she knew US doctors routinely disclose a diagnosis of cancer and she hoped that would be true in her case as well.

'The group could see that this dilemma was a core element of the case, but it wasn't being picked up, so I finally asked, "What about the doc's problem of disclosure? Would you tell the patient she had colon cancer?" For the three men in the group, the answer was a quick "Yes". The two women in the group didn't speak up, but you could see frowns on their faces, suggesting doubt about the quick reply. Nevertheless, the discussion immediately proceeded on to the issue of clinical management of colon cancer. By the end of the tutorial session, the question of disclosure was forgotten. The learning issues they went away with included "staging and screening of colon cancer", "ischemic colitis", "diverticulosis, diverticulitis and diverticular haemorrhage", "pathogenesis and diagnosis of appendicitis" and an overview of "the epidemiology, risk factors, pathogenesis and signs and symptoms of colorectal cancer".

'The students came back to the next tutorial session having thoroughly investigated these issues and they proceeded to efficiently share their learning and apply it to the case. The dilemma faced by the physician in the case was never touched upon again despite an earlier suggestion to the students that they might find useful a particular article about disclosure of a diagnosis of cancer to patients in Japan.

'So, Marlene, what happened to these students over the course of their first year? Why can't we help them sustain their ability to investigate the behavioural components of disease? These Unit 3 students I'm talking about are good students – they work hard and they obviously are caring when it comes to dealing with each other. But I'm worried – here they were faced with a well-written case that included an interesting behavioural issue and they wouldn't pick it up even though they know they will encounter this situation some day on the wards. In Hawaii, with so many elderly patients of Japanese ancestry, there's almost no way to avoid it. What aren't we doing, either as tutors or curriculum designers, to reinforce the perspectives we say are important?'

What do you think are the underlying causes of the situation described?
How would you deal with them?
What do you think should be done next?

PART 2

Gordon and Marlene had discussed this problem many times before. Marlene knows Gordon well and recognized his frustration. She suggested, 'Why don't you go back and talk to those Unit 3 students? See what they think.' Gordon corralled three of the five students from that group as they left a colloquium and asked them if they could help him take a fresh look at an issue that had been bothering him.

The students remembered the problem of the Japanese woman with colon cancer and, with prompting, recalled that her family didn't want the diagnosis disclosed. Gordon asked if they could remember why they didn't investigate this part of the case further. Malia said, 'Dr Greene, be honest. You are really asking why we don't pick up behavioural issues in general. That has always bugged you. I don't know why, but for me, it just doesn't seem like the same kind of learning as investigating the pathophysiology.' Stan was more blunt, 'I agree. You keep saying that there is literature that talks about the ways clinicians can handle these things, but I don't see clinicians referencing that stuff. Nobody talks about it in colloquium and when it shows up in the essay questions on our exams, we just use common sense.' Jesse was somewhat more sympathetic: 'I'm a bit torn. Yes, those things are interesting and sometimes I miss the good discussions we had in Unit 1 about the ways in which people actually experience being sick, but you've got to realize – we just don't have time for that now. There is no payoff.'

The conversation continued in a similar vein, but Gordon still wasn't satisfied. He thought, 'Either we need to find ways to sustain student interest in behavioural issues as part of meaningful learning during the first two years of medical school or we should drop the behavioural perspective from our curriculum goals.' Gordon called Marlene back and relayed the conversation with the former Unit 3 students. 'OK, Marlene, now what?'

If you were a curriculum planner, what steps would you take to try to ensure that a better balance is achieved among important aspects of the curriculum during the students' discussion?
What problems do you think you would encounter if you took these steps and how would you deal with these problems?

PART 3

'Your timing is impeccable, Gordon. I just finished reading the transcript of a focus group we ran with second-year students a few weeks ago. What the second-year students said corroborates what Malia, Stan and Jesse told you. And they went on to say that tutors, too, often give the social sciences short shrift. Can you hold for a minute while I check the transcript for this part of the discussion? – OK, I found it. Let's see – actually, all of the students said pretty much the same thing, so I'll just read one or two of their comments. One student said, "A lot of basic scientists don't realize the implications of behavioural points and emphasize more basic science, and maybe even get side-tracked on some esoteric basic science points." Another continued, "Yeah, that's right. We know we may not need that information to treat patients, but it may be important to know for Boards (a basic science exam required for licensure in the USA), so we want to learn whatever they want to tell us. I think the same is true of clinicians. Sometimes they cover their specialties in too much detail. What they don't get is that they could be role models – people we could ask: how do I choose what I should be focusing on and stuff like that."

'There it is again, Gordon! We both know students are overwhelmed by the amount of biomedical information that's out there. They understand that they can't learn all of it but they're uncertain about what and how much they need to learn to become competent physicians. In a PBL curriculum there's no answer to the question, "How much is enough?" The ambiguity makes students anxious and their anxiety is further fuelled by the Boards which, in their words, "loom just in front of us". It's pretty clear that second-year students see little value or utility in learning about behaviour. And their tutors, whose expertise is in the basic and clinical sciences, often are not prepared to help them approach the social sciences in a rigorous and meaningful way. The point is that faculty and the Boards weight biological knowledge much more heavily than they weight behavioural knowledge, so it is not surprising that students do the same.

'But at least we're trying some things to help students balance their learning of the biomedical and social sciences better. We've rewritten some of the patient cases – and I know that you and a few other tutors try to make the human dimensions of these cases so vivid and compelling that students will recognize that they can no more ignore these dimensions in their discussions and study than they can ignore an infectious agent. We've also rewritten some exam questions – not many, but a few.'

Gordon added, 'Yes, and we've tinkered with other parts of the curriculum, too. Yet, if asked, "Have you succeeded in creating a more patient-centred learning experience for your students?", we would have to answer, "Only a little."'

Marlene agreed.

What other changes might be made to get students to consider issues they do not recognize as important in cases?
What implications does the situation described in this case have for educators who are planning to implement a PBL curriculum at their schools?

CASE REPORTERS' DISCUSSION

The clinical experience our students receive in their first and second years of medical school has been insufficient to counter the strong need they feel to focus on biology. Rewriting a few cases, adding an occasional behavioural question to an exam, and making other small adjustments to the curriculum have not solved our problem. The changes have not motivated students to attend to behavioural issues – issues they still do not consider central to the cases.

The question we face is, 'How can we help students learn material we know is important in a context where they have the prerogative to say that other learning is more important?' Of course, one option open to us is to drop the curriculum goal of learning behavioural concepts in the pre-clinical years. This would end the struggle, but it also would undermine our educational philosophy, which emphasizes the importance of learning about the whole patient from the first day of medical school. Another option is to renew our commitment to our educational philosophy and the study of behavioural concepts, and make more profound changes to the pre-clinical curriculum. To do this, we think that as curriculum planners we might take the following steps:

- Enlist the support of upper level administrators and senior faculty and even ask them if they would publicly reaffirm the goal of learning behavioural concepts in the first and second years of medical school, thereby redirecting institutional focus toward the integration of the biomedical and social sciences.
- Develop a range of educational sessions, including workshops that focus specifically on the knowledge and skills necessary to sustain attention to the behavioural perspective of medicine throughout all years of the curriculum. Demonstrate that there are specific skills to be learnt for interacting with patients – skills that are not based on intuition or common sense but are grounded in the humanities as well as the social sciences. More importantly, emphasize the solid and growing body of clinical literature that demonstrates that attention to the behavioural components of medicine is not simply 'kind' or 'interesting' but often has a significant – and sometimes critical – impact on the outcome of an illness for a patient.
- Engage faculty who have knowledge of behavioural issues in the review of patient cases. Rewrite cases as needed to incorporate important social science concepts. Include a list of relevant clinical and social science references in the cases.
- Reward students' understanding of social science literature by assessing knowledge, skills and attitudes related to behavioural concepts discussed in this literature. Include a representative number of behavioural items on tests and performance assessments. If we do not emphasize behavioural concepts in assessment, we are teaching students that these concepts are not important, a point quickly recognized by students.
- Guide the intended curriculum change by systematically evaluating learning experiences, learning materials and assessment instruments.
- Close the loop by communicating evaluation findings to administrators, faculty and students.

Taking these steps would relieve unit chairs, tutors and case writers of the need to add increasing baggage to the PBL cases. Instead, the responsibility for emphasizing the care and well-being of the whole patient would be distributed more evenly across all components of the curriculum.

Although this case study deals with a specific dilemma at our medical school, an analogous problem might arise in a PBL curriculum in any discipline at any educational level. We believe that, to address this problem effectively, the entire curriculum, not just the PBL cases, must reinforce the learning that curriculum planners perceive as central but students do not yet recognize as essential to their education.

CHAPTER 12

REDESIGNING PBL: RESOLVING THE INTEGRATION PROBLEM

Case reporters: Barry Maitland and Rob Cowdroy

Issues raised

This case study begins with the issue of translating a PBL model from one discipline to another and then focuses on the integration of knowledge and learning, which came to be seen as a key feature of the new model.

Background

The architecture course at the University of Newcastle in New South Wales is one of some 15 professionally accredited architecture schools in Australia, and one of only a few located outside the state capital cities. It has a tradition of regarding itself as a distinctive institution, with a strong practice focus and strong regional as well as international links.

The course is run by the Department of Architecture within the Faculty of Architecture, Building and Design and has an enrolment of almost 300 students. The Bachelor of Architecture (BArch) degree qualification is accredited as the formal education part of requirements for professional registration of architects under state legislation. The course is planned and facilitated by 10 full-time teaching staff, plus three on fractional appointments, and 20 sessional teachers, including several postgraduate tutors.

PART 1

In the mid-1980s, after a period of instability and doubts over its future, the School of Architecture at the University of Newcastle was ready for change.

The mood for change and renewal was motivated partly by a desire to reinvigorate the architecture programme and partly by the perception that, in order to survive, the school had to enhance its distinctive profile in competition with the larger metropolitan architecture schools, particularly the three in Sydney. This created a general willingness among all the staff to contemplate innovation and change but no clear idea about what form that change should take. There was, of course, the highly regarded model on campus of the recently formed medical school, which was fresh from its initial exhilarating stages of establishing its pioneering PBL course, but we architects did not immediately see this as necessarily relevant to our situation.

Our first step, then, was a period of critical self-evaluation, to attempt to articulate exactly what our shortcomings and limitations were. We held a series of workshops and seminars at which each staff member in turn prepared a discussion paper on one aspect of the course, leading to general discussion. The critique began at a rather detailed and piecemeal level ('I think we spend too much time teaching European architectural history', 'We should have more field trips', etc). Gradually, however, it broadened to consider how other architecture schools both in Australia and overseas handled similar issues, and finally it came to focus on a few key problems and two in particular.

The first was the question of relevance. How could a small and comparatively isolated architecture school keep in touch with the greater currents of change and innovation constantly transforming the architectural profession worldwide? And even at a local level, how could we determine what actually was a relevant education for a prospective architect in our region?

The second fundamental problem that kept recurring in debate was the classic difficulty of all architecture schools in overcoming the separation between different strands of the curriculum, and in particular the basic division between that part of the course conducted in the design studio and the remainder in the traditional university settings of lecture theatre and laboratory. This typically leads to an almost schizophrenic duality, with the former seen by students as creative, relevant and sexy, and the latter as dull, exam-driven and remote from 'real' architecture. The symptoms of this separation are commonplace in all architecture schools. The lecturer in structures, for example, wonders: 'Why is it that students who are working on a project in the design studio seem to remember nothing of what I told them last year about just such a problem?' Typically the response to this incomprehensible failure is the setting up of a staff committee to more closely coordinate the different strands, but without noticeable benefit.

At this point we began to take a closer look at the Newcastle medical model. We discovered that that model had been devised precisely to address similar problems of relevance and curriculum fragmentation. We invited staff from medicine to talk to us about their approach and with some trepidation considered their advice that, of course, the model would work equally well for us.

But would it? The natures of the two disciplines were very different. The medical course was concerned with discovery and diagnosis, whereas architecture was about invention and finding responses to problems for which there was no 'correct' solution. Might the medical model prove to be a disastrously expensive dead-end for us? By chance we became aware at this time of an author who was exploring the differences between ways of thinking and problem solving in different professions, and whose ideas offered encouragement to our tentative steps forward. In *The Reflective Practitioner* and subsequently *The Design Studio*, Donald Schön (1983, 1985) discusses the differences between the 'convergent' thinking of the 'hard' sciences and the 'divergent' thinking of the 'soft' professions, and the strategies the latter have developed to cope with the intractable, 'wicked' problems they have to address. He points to the architecture design studio in particular as a potent model of this form of dynamic problem solving. Indeed, he goes so far as to suggest that other professions, especially the 'hard', 'major' professions, should consider this model as an alternative to their customary educational forms.

This was refreshing stuff, and paradoxical in the sense that the tendency among many architecture schools was to abandon the studio in favour of the lecture theatre/laboratory settings of the more prestigious, 'hard' university disciplines. Schön's idea, coupled with the admirable clarity of the medical PBL insistence on the centrality of the 'problem' as the only way to generate an integrated problem-solving environment, gave us the confidence to contemplate a completely integrated PBL architecture first-year course for the following year, 1985, to be based on a succession of studio-centred projects/problems that would be the sole generators of all supporting lecture, laboratory and field-work presentations. But we were faced with a major decision: how would we go about adapting the medical PBL model to our own very different discipline?

What do you think might be the most important features that would have to be changed from the medical model of PBL to meet the needs of the architecture programme?
What features of the medical model of PBL should not be changed?
What specific aspects of the design and delivery of the new PBL course would these most affect?

PART 2

One of the most striking features of the medical course to our eyes was the short duration of their problem phases compared to our design projects. Presumably there is a special urgency about medical problems, but the difference also seemed to reflect the different nature of the processes of the two disciplines. The time cycle of the customary medical problem, from presentation through research and analysis to the testing of alternative hypotheses, seemed inevitably more abbreviated than that of architectural projects. Partly this could be attributed to the more laborious and time-consuming processes of drawing, modelling and testing the architectural proposal, but partly also there seemed to be a longer span involved in arriving at satisfactory solutions that would fully integrate the various social, cultural, economic, environmental, aesthetic and technical dimensions of the architectural problem.

This issue would also have a bearing on the forms of assessment used, for whereas the medical programme had devised a number of tests separate from the sequence of problems to gauge students' performance, it seemed to us that the only way to assess our core attribute of 'design integration' (that is, the resolution in a design of the demands of all those disparate dimensions) would be from the extended design phases themselves.

As a result of these considerations, we adopted the basic principles and characteristics of the medical PBL model, but the pattern of problem phases was substantially modified to much longer blocks, and the assessment system was heavily weighted to continuous assessment of the design phases. To ensure this, we allocated 50 per cent of the overall assessment for a year's programme to performance in design integration, and 50 per cent to performance in individual study areas, with a requirement that students achieve an adequate standard in each.

The first year of the five-year architecture programme was converted to the new model in 1985, with such an enthusiastic response that students at a later stage in the course demanded that they too be accommodated. Accordingly, both the second and fourth years were converted in 1986 and the third and fifth in 1987.

For staff, one of the crucial measures of our success was the response to the 'integration problem'. This was where we had our first hint that not all of the goals of the curricular change were being met. When the PBL approach was applied to the fourth and fifth years in particular, the teaching staff became aware that, while integration of the curriculum had been achieved, integration of previous learning was not so successful. In particular, students were having difficulty applying what they had learnt earlier in the course (PBL or otherwise) to the more complex projects (problems) encountered in the later stages of the course.

The students were highly focused on the problems and on the information being presented at that time, but they were not integrating knowledge and skills that they had previously acquired. When prompted, students were able to recall previous learning and, when pressed, they recognized its relevance to their present projects. However, students were dismayed when they were penalized for not spontaneously considering and applying this previous learning.

This prior learning might have been considered surface learning except that the recall after prompting was reasonably comprehensive. The previous learning seemed to have been deep enough, but the students' approach to the projects themselves appeared to be shallow (surface?). The students also appeared to be depending on the teachers, particularly their group tutors, for expansion of the project beyond what was explicitly given or set, eg as a trigger.

We recognized that this was in conflict with the facilitation role of group tutors that was a particular tenet of PBL. We also recognized that it was in conflict with the notion of reflection that was a focus of Schön's writings. This phenomenon also was in conflict with a more general shift in educational focus from teacher-centred to student-centred learning processes.

We had expected integration and reflection to follow from the application of PBL in the small-group, studio teaching environment and these conflicts were a considerable concern to us. Our concern translated into dissatisfaction with student performance and was met by student dissatisfaction with their teachers' lack of enthusiasm for what the students saw as good work that met the requirements of the problems as set.

From the students' viewpoint, the criteria for recognition of good work were not sufficiently defined for them to work towards, and the teachers appeared to be applying arbitrary standards. From the teachers' viewpoint, students should have 'known' to apply earlier learning to their present work without having to be told. To not do so suggested naivety and/or poor earlier learning and/or laziness. The teachers were concerned that the general standard of student performance was below what was required for them to enter the profession. In short, the students were being 'unprofessional'.

Furthermore, we were having trouble getting the students to participate in groups. Some of the weakest students absented themselves out of frustration with the group process, while some of the strongest students stayed away because of the slow pace and intellectual mediocrity of the groups. We had a problem on our hands. How could we get the groups back on track and also get the students to do the sort of 'integrating' of knowledge and skills that we had hoped to achieve with the change to PBL?

What sorts of steps do you think could be taken to deal with these problems? What do you think actually was done and what sorts of effects did the measures have?

PART 3

Two teachers with strong management backgrounds analysed the situation in the light of Schön's writings. To them, the difficulty was a failure of the individual student to 'think like a professional', to view a project holistically as a practitioner would, and to apply professional standards of both pragmatic and intellectual rigour to the given work. Hence, to solve the dilemma and have the student 'think like a professional', each student should analyse and question the project as given, integrate previous learning and common sense with acquired professional skills, and develop and communicate an individual solution.

Furthermore, again based on Schön's writing, we recognized the importance of the 'conceptual design' approach to design teaching in architectural education. The conceptual design approach is a reflective one in which many possible hypothesized outcomes are successively tested against increasingly complex criteria including function, structural sufficiency, environmental impact and defensibility on both pragmatic and intellectual dimensions. Here, every individual student in the group is expected to develop his or her own preferred outcome according to the criteria applied by the individual and his or her ranking of those criteria. This individualistic emphasis in architectural education reflects the individualistic ethos of the profession and differs from the consensus emphasis assumed for medicine in the PBL literature.

We realized that, in this scenario, the group tutorial would have to serve a different purpose from what had originally been envisaged. It would be a forum for discussion of students' individual approaches and solutions, rather than for development of 'agreed' group approaches as espoused in the PBL literature. This individualization of the group activity, however, was more suited to the traditional modus operandi of the architectural profession than were the PBL conventions that were (and still are) heavily biased towards assumptions about the medical profession.

This, then, appeared to be the solution to the integration problem: reinforce the conceptual design process (which underlies all architectural education) to achieve the necessary integration in the mind of the student. In order to do this, each individual student must integrate a wide range of disparate knowledge and skills. Also, each student must be prepared to defend not only the proposed solution, but also the criteria and the ranking of the criteria, which have become the 'envelope' of his or her solution, and the criteria for the evaluation of the proposed solution.

At the same time, we recognized the value of the group process, particularly for developing social and teamworking skills, and for sharing some of the common information-gathering demands of complex projects. We therefore moved towards a duplex system: 'work as a group/think individually'. Evaluating the individual focused on evaluating integration, and the 'present and defend' approach shifted the focus of evaluation from the proposal itself (as evidence of student ability to arrive at a solution) to the reasoning by which the student had arrived at that proposal (as evidence of the student's ability to integrate and apply all the relevant philosophical, theoretical and technical considerations into a single complex solution). Nevertheless, a student could not achieve a satisfactory outcome without group interaction, cooperation, debate and support, so the group remained important to achieving both individual outcomes and the corporate educational objectives.

This modification of our PBL approach to a more individualistic emphasis had a profound impact on the character of the programme, with much greater ownership by students of the problems/projects and outcomes and, consequently, much greater enthusiasm and motivation of students to be professional in their approaches to their own projects. The success of this approach was almost immediately seen in the much higher standard of work by all students and the outstanding success of students and graduates in competition for state and national awards, and in competition for preferred employment.

What are the lessons from this case for other disciplines that are thinking of adopting PBL? What changes from the medical model need to be considered? What are the implications of the integration issue? How can students be helped to develop the ability to integrate their early PBL learning into what they do later in the course?

CASE REPORTERS' DISCUSSION

At the heart of this case study are the challenges we faced, first of all, to adapt a medical model of PBL to a very different discipline and, then, to further adapt PBL to suit the realities of architectural practice. Initially, some of us had difficulty 'handing over' control of the projects and the selection of criteria for students' evaluation. With experience, however, we became increasingly enthusiastic about the new 'professional' atmosphere, and this enthusiasm soon affected all staff and encouraged a symbiotic enthusiasm and confidence between students and staff.

Indeed, one interpretation of this development could be that it represented a progression from a strongly teacher-structured and controlled version of PBL to a more student-centred approach, and this raised the question of what other features of our model might benefit from the same shift. Or, to put it another way, what alternative steps might we have taken to achieve a similar result?

From the beginning we had been aware that the operation of the new PBL model was restricted by shortage of studio space, such that most students had only shared access for restricted periods. This tended to reinforce the impression of the studio as a classroom associated with passive, teacher-directed activity. Increasingly, we became convinced that student-centred learning would be greatly enhanced by providing a more effective setting in which students could themselves experiment with different patterns of interaction and work without timetable restrictions, much as happens in the world of architectural practice. In response to this, the university, impressed by the successes of the course, agreed to build a new studio facility for the architecture school in 1994, providing a workspace for every architecture student from all years together in the same space, with student access on a 24-hour, 7-day-a-week basis.

This development had a further profound impact on the character of the programme. The building was seen as 'belonging' to the students, with staff entering in the role of facilitators and supporters in conformity with the ideals of PBL. The sometimes chaotic informality of the studio allowed a greater degree of self-pacing and time management by students, exposing novice students to the work practices and ways of thinking of experienced students, and allowing minorities, particularly from overseas, to form mutual support groups under the general umbrella.

Rather than undermining the PBL model, our reinterpretation of the medical PBL approach resolved the integration problem and allowed the course to flourish with a renewed vigour that is reflected in the consistently high level of accreditation given to the course. In reflecting on this success, we are reminded that education ultimately occurs in the mind of the student, and that the physical environment and setting play an important part, beyond the philosophical issues with which we had been so preoccupied.

References

Schön, D A (1983) *The Reflective Practitioner: How professionals think in action*, Basic Books, New York

Schön, D A (1985) *The Design Studio: An exploration of its traditions and potentials*, RIBA Publications, London

CHAPTER 13

WHY DOES THE DEPARTMENT HAVE PROFESSORS IF THEY DON'T TEACH?

Case reporters: Barbara Miflin and David Price

Issues raised

This case study looks at how confusion about the concept of self-directed learning can cause difficulties during the implementation of a problem-based curriculum, and at how this confusion can be addressed.

Background

The Graduate Medical Course (GMC) commenced at the School of Medicine, The University of Queensland, in 1997 (although the Medical School was established over 60 years earlier). It is a four-year, graduate entry, problem-based course, leading to the award of the Bachelor of Medicine/Bachelor of Surgery (MBBS) degree. Class size is 240 students per year. The teaching staff consists of approximately 1000 individuals in 12 academic departments and approximately 1500 visiting and consultant staff, mostly involved in clinical teaching. Before the innovation, the medical course followed the British tradition (six years long, comprising three pre-clinical years and three clinical years).

PART 1

The authors of this case constitute the Academic Staff Development Unit (ASDU) in the School of Medicine. We have responsibility for preparing teaching staff for the GMC. Both of us have educational backgrounds; we are not medically qualified. Recognizing that we did not 'speak the language' of medicine, we started by using the few medically qualified academics with prior experience in PBL from elsewhere as our frontline 'trainers'. Since 1996, approximately 500 PBL tutors have been trained.

Given the size of the class, some of the resources students use to address the learning objectives they generate in PBL sessions are organized as large-group exercises, for example lectures, 'expert'-led tutorials, practical (laboratory) classes and clinical skills sessions in the hospitals. These are presented in a standard type of timetable that intersects with the PBL tutorial sessions. We also provided initial training workshops, using academic staff as 'trainers', for staff who were to deliver resources.

Early in the first year of the new course, we discovered that there was confusion about the concept of student self-direction in the new curriculum. We understood that 'self-direction' in a PBL curriculum means essentially that what the learning students do is based in and driven by the learning deficiencies they identify when trying to address a patient 'problem'. However, many teachers and curriculum leaders in the GMC interpreted 'self-direction' quite differently, including those who designed the curriculum and those we had used to train others.

As early as the third week of the first year, students complained that they were 'being expected to teach ourselves medicine' and that 'in this course, students have to do everything'. They asked questions such as: 'Why does the department have professors if they don't teach?' Student comments were directed mainly at resource sessions, specifically lectures, 'expert' tutorials and laboratory classes. Students expected to be able to get expert teaching in these sessions to address the learning objectives they generated from 'problem' discussion. However, many resource providers seemed to have a different view and, instead of teaching students, either posed extra 'problems' for students to 'solve' for themselves (in lectures and 'expert' tutorials) or simply provided resource material, such as anatomical or pathological specimens, and no guidance or instruction on how they were to be used. For example, in the department responsible for major resource provision in Year 1, demonstrators in laboratory-based practical classes were instructed not to answer students' questions, no instruction was provided to students on how to work with specimens, and the 'professors' in the department were available in their offices at set times during the week if students wanted to see them about the discipline! Remember that there were 240 students in the year.

PBL tutors were unsure about how much 'direction' to provide. Most had not given students any guidance in how to 'do' PBL. They were reluctant to intervene in the learning process, believing that their task was to facilitate (a term with a great deal of air play at the time) self-directed learning by adopting a low profile in the group and letting students 'discover' the process for themselves. This was considered appropriate for 'adult learners' (yet another popular notion).

In trying to explain why students were unhappy, staff who found the whole notion of change difficult made comments such as: 'What do you expect when her undergraduate degree is in music (or engineering or nursing or law or teaching)?' Others suggested that the students were simply lazy, arrogant or 'just plain stupid'.

On the other hand, teachers who supported reform were shocked and disappointed in the students' attitudes. They expected that graduate students, especially mature-age students (as many in the first cohort were), would appreciate the opportunity to direct their own learning in all aspects of the course. In looking for explanations, teachers blamed the didactic nature of students' prior educational experiences for making them dependent on direction by teachers. Alternatively, they argued that students lacked confidence because they had been away from formal study for too long. Most argued that PBL meant students should be prepared to use the resources put at their disposal to 'teach themselves'. In other words, they equated self-direction in PBL curricula with 'discovery' learning of everything, not just discovery of what one needed to learn.

Since that first year, we have found that the notion that self-direction is achieved by self-teaching is widespread and is almost always connected in teachers' minds with the concepts of 'adult learning' and 'facilitation'. Although fine sentiments in themselves, these concepts were often hazily understood, and rarely were the principles underlying them articulated. Not surprisingly, there was confusion about their meaning, and the confusion was transferred to the interpretation of these concepts in the problem-based curriculum.

The danger was that achievement of the goal of self-direction and the other benefits of PBL might be lost. Instead of learning in an environment that gave them confidence in their own choices, students became angry and frustrated, many became dependent on direct faculty guidance, and some withdrew from the PBL tutorial process, reverting to rote learning based on textbooks to cope with the uncertainty. How were we going to influence the 'change' (and the 'changers') towards a more appropriate interpretation of these fundamental concepts?

Given that the prime movers of reform in the School had spent months working to design and develop the curriculum on the basis of their understanding of problem-based learning, getting them to reconsider was not going to be easy. For those who had worked tirelessly for innovation, reputations and, more importantly, self-esteem were involved.

And it was not just a teaching issue. Conceptual confusion had infected the curricular design. It was futile to try to change approaches to teaching based on a new understanding when what was to be taught and learnt was based on a different understanding.

As staff developers, we had a defined role. How could we deliver the message? How urgent was the task? What could we do?

If you were in our position, how would you proceed?
What are the key issues that need to be addressed?
How would you address the students' concerns?

PART 2

We believed that the only way to proceed was to encourage faculty to reflect on these issues as soon as possible.

In our reports on case studies of resource provision to the GMC by two departments, we explored the concepts of 'discovery learning' and self-direction, clarified the meaning of self-directed learning as we understood it in problem-based curricula, and recommended that the departments reconsider their approach to teaching. Both departments made changes. We sought permission from the heads of these departments to send copies of our reports to heads of the other departments involved in the GMC. We discussed our findings with the Head of the School of Medicine.

Not surprisingly, the reports had limited impact on other departments. With the Head of School, however, we developed a conceptual framework about the development of self-direction in the GMC. In essence, we proposed that self-direction for lifelong learning is a goal (one product) of a problem-based curriculum rather than the entire learning process by which it is achieved. Students 'direct' their own learning by identifying learning objectives from 'problems'. When they are able to address their learning deficits effectively by accessing, inter alia, the expertise in content and in teaching that resides in the faculty and the profession, they become confident in their own decision making about learning. The best of conventional teaching, rather than being antithetical to the development of self-direction through PBL, is actually a necessity.

We revised material used in staff development activities to stress this message, particularly the role of active teaching in the GMC, and we made sure we explained the refined concept of self-direction in continuing activities, especially in PBL tutor training. We stressed the importance of guidance early in students' PBL experience and of strategic intervention subsequently to maintain an effective process. Tutors and students report that these changes have revived confidence in the curriculum. However, misinterpretation of what 'self-direction' means persists in some quarters.

To address the underlying curricular design issues, we encouraged the Head of School to invite experienced external consultants to advise the Curriculum Committee. The 'visitors' provided practical assistance in review of the PBL cases, resulting in effective revision of their content and format. Students report that case discussion in PBL tutorials is far more effective and that they have more confidence that they are identifying relevant learning objectives. Combined with improved teaching in resource sessions, this means that students have more confidence in directing their own learning.

What other methods might have been used to improve insight about the meaning of 'self-direction'?
What would you do differently?

CASE REPORTERS' DISCUSSION

Despite the size of the task facing the faculty in Queensland, there were very many positive achievements, and those involved – teachers and students – found the new approach refreshing and enjoyable.

The lessons? We suggest to readers that they take care to understand that the beliefs and presuppositions of teachers about teaching and learning are powerful and that very subtle forces can interfere with effective curricular change and remain for the most part unarticulated (Miflin *et al*, 1999). We urge others to avoid the mistake we made in not recognizing early enough that notions such as self-directed learning, adult learning and discovery learning, while they were bandied about, were not explored properly. Teachers, including those we used in training others, interpreted these notions differently, depending on the level of their teaching experience, acceptance of the need for change and, as Egan (1978) argues, their essential worldview, including whether students (human beings) are essentially 'good' or 'bad', trustworthy or not. Because there had been so many teachers to prepare, staff development was considerably under-resourced, and because teachers could not be released from ongoing duties for more than a few hours, these notions were not addressed and explored in training. In hindsight, had we taken more time initially, much of our later work in redressing misconceptions would have been unnecessary. To address these issues now, we use the conceptual framework about self-direction to guide curriculum revision, teacher preparation, assessment and evaluation. A detailed description was published recently (Miflin *et al*, 2000). For the seminal work on self-direction in tertiary education, we recommend *Self-direction for Lifelong Learning* (Candy, 1991).

Thankfully, we know from student feedback that the very maturity of the first cohort, especially experience in the professional workplace, meant that these students coped better than most students would with the 'teething troubles' of the new curriculum. Students certainly appreciated the efforts so many teachers made to understand and address their concerns. We hope that readers can learn from our experience how important it is to seek feedback from students and teachers, to monitor their concerns and to trust their instincts about anomalies in the implementation of new curricula.

A further lesson is to encourage teachers to reflect together. Schumacher (1977) advises that we all need each other to be adequate for the tasks we undertake. Exploration of educational ideas is generally alien to the tertiary environment. Dialogue about educational issues is certainly not commonplace in medical faculties, although the impetus for reform is strong. The reasons are many and well recognized. Among them are the constraints exerted by political and resource considerations, the conservative reaction of the profession and the lack of specific or formal preparation of teaching staff in education. We ensure that PBL tutors reflect not only on the 'content' of PBL cases but also on the PBL process in our regular briefing/debriefing meetings. Our annual curriculum conference always incorporates reflection on progress. We have learnt that external expertise is invaluable for guiding the initial stages of curricular change and is also an essential catalyst for reflection.

The final message is to have patience, think laterally and don't give up hope. Although feeling frustrated at times, we have learnt that the innovative environment is unparalleled for stimulating the type of educational dialogue and reflectivity in teachers that is generally missing from the tertiary sphere. The ultimate result for students is a better education and, for the rest of us, doctors who are personally secure, professionally sound and prepared to continue to learn throughout their careers.

References

Candy, P (1991) *Self-direction for Lifelong Learning*, Jossey-Bass, San Francisco, CA

Egan, K (1978) 'Some presuppositions that determine curriculum decisions', *Curriculum Studies*, 10 (2): 123–33

Miflin, B M, Campbell, C B and Price, D A (1999) 'A lesson from the introduction of a problem-based, graduate entry course: the effects of different views of self-direction', *Medical Education*, 33, 801–07

Miflin, B M, Campbell, C B and Price, D A (2000) 'A conceptual framework to guide the development of self-directed, lifelong learning in problem-based medical curricula', *Medical Education*, 34, 299–306

Schumacher, E (1977) *A Guide for the Perplexed*, Jonathan Cape, London

CHAPTER 14

FACULTY DEVELOPMENT WORKSHOPS: A 'CHALLENGE' OF PROBLEM-BASED LEARNING?

Case reporters: Deborah E Allen, Barbara J Duch and Susan E Groh

Issues raised

This case focuses on the issue of dealing with difficulties arising during faculty development workshops on PBL as a result of different attitudes, ideas, goals and levels of experience among participants. In this example, the difficulties arise in the context of a consideration of assessment in PBL.

Background

In 1996, several faculty members at a medium-sized, graduate degree granting university in the United States created an institute (the Institute for Instructional Innovation) whose major goal is to encourage faculty to adopt active group learning strategies such as PBL in their undergraduate courses. Two week-long series of workshops led by the Institute founders inform and guide the faculty participants (Institute Fellows) as they learn how to implement these strategies in their own classrooms.

PART 1

It was the fourth day of the workshop series and Sarah, one of the workshop leaders, faced the morning with a sinking feeling in her stomach. The topic for the day's two-and-a-half-hour opening session was assessment of student learning, and it was her turn to take the lead role. As she went over the plans for the session while drinking her second coffee of the morning, she was anxious. She takes up the story.

I knew that it was likely to be a challenge. Right from the first day of this workshop series I saw that we had participants with the typical mix of motivations for taking part in the sessions and with the usual variability in levels of understanding of what PBL is all about. There was the worrier about loss of coverage of content, the teacher who confused PBL with problem solving, the faculty member who thought most students were inherently lazy and wouldn't take to PBL, the one who was concerned about how much time PBL would take away from her research, the teacher looking for a way to use PBL for a large enrolment course – and even the one who had used PBL for several years already and styled himself as an expert. How would such a group deal with assessment, a thorny enough issue without bringing in the additional baggage of scepticism, anxiety and uncertainty about PBL?

I must admit that my first thoughts were, 'Why did I agree to take this on? Why did I think I could do any better than the experts on assessment who have tried to "pull off" these sessions in the past? Just a lot of preaching to the converted, with hardly any impact on the truly resistant or "not quite there yet" contingent. What's the average time until the first questioner inevitably derails the whole workshop session? About 20 minutes?'

I relaxed when I recognized that my plan for the session seemed to be sound: to start by giving some basic pointers about assessment strategies, particularly on the importance of matching them to one's objectives for student learning, followed by some seasoned Institute Fellows from previous years sharing their favourite strategies with this year's new Fellows.

An hour later, I was briefly introducing 'Bloom's Taxonomy' of cognitive levels. 'So far, so good', I thought. Addressing the group, I said, 'I have a short assignment I'd like you to work on. Remember we asked you to bring your objectives for the course you'd like to transform to PBL, or to think about what they might be for the new PBL course that you're designing. Take a look at your course objectives, and decide how you could assess the extent to which students are making progress towards accomplishing them.'

Later, during the reporting out sessions, the first difficult moment of the day occurred. I was listening to Liz, a Fellow from the psychology department, recounting her list of learning objectives for her course, and my impression was that they all seemed to go no further than requiring students to understand the finer points of course content. I thought, 'What shall I say to her when she's done? How can I break it to her gently that she seems to have missed the point of my introduction?'

When Liz finished presenting her course objectives, she said to the room, 'I have to confess, I couldn't think of any way to test students other than what I'm already doing, which is to give multiple-choice exams. I thought about asking some more difficult and complicated questions in an essay format, but I'm worried about how I'll have the time to grade 300 essays, even short ones. I've really enjoyed trading ideas with my group members about how they go about testing students in their departments, but since no one is from psychology, I didn't get much useful advice. Sorry, folks…'.

Before I could even get a word in, Jim from chemistry piped up: 'One thing I do in my large-enrolment chemistry course is to assign homework problems from the end of the textbook chapter. Once students hand them in, I just scan the papers quickly, then give each student a "check" for having turned one in. Then I post the right answers on my course Web site.'

'I do that, too,' chimed in Ann from physics, 'but I think the question you asked us to answer about our course objectives misses the point. All morning I've been waiting for you to tell us just how we can teach our students critical thinking skills, but I haven't heard anything yet that's useful. I'm looking for a step-by-step method that I can actually use in my classical mechanics course. What's the point of asking students challenging questions in an exam if you haven't taught them how to go about thinking that way? If that's not what this session is about, is there a book you can give me that can help me learn how to do this?'

Here were all the old doubts, confusions, preconceptions and anxieties cropping up, this time in the context of assessment. To top it all off, before I could begin to compose a reply to Jim and Ann's concerns, let alone comment on Liz's presentation, Ken, the teacher from biology who had some 'expertise' in PBL, started to speak. 'I agree that this session misses the point, but that's not it. You can't teach critical thinking skills – I thought everyone knew that already. My problem is that I think this whole idea of setting up a matrix to follow up on every detail of what the course instructor wants the students to learn is so anti-PBL. The whole point is to let the students identify what they need to learn from the process. I know my students would be completely turned off if I tried to box them in this way. Let me tell you about this exam I give called a triple jump…'. He started to move towards the front of the room.

All eyes turned to me, wondering how I would respond. I looked at my colleagues from the Institute and sensed that distinct 'here we go again' look in their eyes. Gulp – I was in the hot seat – it was up to me to deal with the situation.

What underlying themes are driving the concerns expressed by Liz, Jim, Ann and Ken?
What advice can you offer Sarah on how to respond to get this session back on track? How should she respond, if at all, to Liz, Jim, Ann and Ken's concerns?

PART 2

I decided to keep my cool, but that it was time to take control and to stick to the plan that I had worked out for the session. I stopped Ken before he reached the front of the room, reminding him that we had a series of guest presenters waiting to talk about their assessment strategies. Then I replied briefly to the issues that had been raised, validating these concerns, and I assured everyone that there would be time at the end of the session to have a deeper discussion of these issues. I said, 'Liz, the presenters will show you some good ideas for assessing, and I can give you references to some useful resources. The consensus from previous workshops has been that, while it is difficult to assess students' ability to apply and analyse in a multiple-choice exam format, it's not impossible. In fact, I thought this point might arise and I've got an example to show you in the last part of the session. Jim, your ideas on how to handle additional assignments in your large class sound good, but there are other possibilities. Another approach to giving feedback might be to use some of your class time to give examples of the different approaches that students had used to find a similar solution to the problems you assigned. And Ann, that's a good point about skills in critical thinking. During the upcoming mid-session break, why don't you all think about what experiences, both in and out of the classroom, were of most benefit in helping you develop a capacity for higher order thinking? Then we can discuss your ideas.'

Finally, I dealt with Ken's concern about the tension between student-centred learning and teacher direction in PBL and its assessment. I said, 'I can see your point, Ken, but I think there are ways around the dilemma. For example, one strategy that works well to both preserve PBL's student-centred nature and permit "authentic" assessment is for the course instructor to state the overall objectives of the course in a general way at the start of the semester, and then to give an overview of the ways in which students progress towards meeting each of them will be assessed. As they work on individual PBL problems, students will have the opportunity to identify the learning issues that will help them move towards the problem resolution. Then as each problem reaches its resolution, the instructor can provide a more specific description of objectives and assessment mechanisms linked to that problem. That way students can be made aware of what the course designer had in mind when choosing the particular problem.'

After that, everybody seemed to settle down, so at least that part of my response was successful. And we had lots of good discussion and sharing of ideas. Whether it all made any difference, though, would require a mind reader – or someone sitting in on these Fellows' classes in the future! What I do know from the workshop evaluations is that the participants appreciated having this forum to air their anxieties about changing their teaching, and they left at the end of the week satisfied and enthusiastic about putting some of the workshop ideas into practice – not necessarily to try PBL, but to change some aspects of the way they teach to incorporate more student-active (or less instructor-centred) approaches. Almost all of them said they would recommend the workshop experience to their colleagues.

How well do you feel the situation was handled?
What other options might Sarah have tried?
What other methods might be considered for PBL workshops for faculty development?

CASE REPORTERS' DISCUSSION

The Institute for Instructional Innovation attracts participants for a variety of reasons. Many of them bring expectations, concerns and misconceptions about the programme and about PBL. The participants' concerns noted by Sarah early in Part 1 are typical. All are understandable in faculty who are coming to grips with unfamiliar and non-traditional teaching methods like PBL. For this case we have chosen to focus on the example of assessment to illustrate the sorts of views that might be expressed by participants and the approaches that might be taken to address the issues and to work with the participants.

As seen in the case study, a session leader needs to be continuously aware of and adept at validating the concerns expressed by participants, while at the same time keeping a mind's eye on the ultimate goals and needs of all participants. Flexibility on the part of the session facilitator – a willingness and ability to make continual, minor adjustments to the anticipated schedule of activities in the interest of accomplishing the broader goals – is essential. Sarah faced a difficulty, however, that limited her ability to lead a discussion of the points raised by the participants. Included in her session schedule were presentations by colleagues of their successful assessment strategies for PBL classes, and she had to ensure they had their allotted time while still responding to the concerns expressed by participants and providing opportunity for further discussion of them later. Sarah appears to have dealt with this aspect of the dilemma satisfactorily.

Issues related to assessment will test the skills of even the best workshop leaders. These issues are of such overwhelming concern to faculty engaged in any educational change process that they tend to resurface no matter how perceptive and otherwise gifted the workshop session leaders are. Anxieties over content coverage and perceived loss of control over the classroom agenda (among other key issues) inevitably seem to arise in sessions on assessment of student learning in a PBL context.

Why is this so? Beyond the obvious issues of power, governance and control, it is here that faculty are most confronted by an apparent contradiction between what they acknowledge is the overall goal of the college/university experience – to increase students' critical thinking skills – and the opportunities provided by traditional course activities and assessment strategies for students to make progress towards this goal. Faculty may, for the first time, recognize that their often lofty aims for student learning are not reflected in what they are holding students accountable for via the assessment methods they have been using.

Liz's comments in Part 1 reflect the anxieties often felt by faculty teaching large enrolment courses when they find that assessment in PBL may well require the use of some additional and perhaps new assessment tools beyond those that evaluate students' recall and understanding of course content. Sarah did well in dealing briefly with the concerns that many of the workshop participants no doubt shared with Liz. The useful resources Sarah could point participants to for a deeper look at assessment strategies include Anderson and Speck, 1998; Angelo and Cross, 1993 and Rogers and Sando, 1996.

Alternatively, the participants can receive practical advice on assessment from their peers who face the same classroom conditions. One way that we have found successful at our workshops to address the concerns about assessment methods is to incorporate presentations by former Institute Fellows. The ones that have a particularly strong impact are those that provide creative strategies for how these assessment mechanisms can be used in a large enrolment class setting without excessive demands on faculty time.

Jim's ideas for how to handle additional assignments in a large class are basically sound and Sarah affirmed this. She might want to emphasize in her suggested alternative method that certain end-of-chapter questions might support such an approach, while others might undo some of the goals of PBL by reinforcing a 'plug-and-chug' or 'pattern-matching' strategy to finding a single 'right' answer. At Institute workshops, we also commonly pose the question: does all assessment need to be linked to a grade? By doing so we introduce a discussion of pre- and formative assessment.

Sarah's suggestion that participants reflect on the experiences that helped them develop a capacity for higher order thinking could lead to a good discussion at the end of the entire workshop week about the pros and cons of lecture versus active learning in achieving the goal of helping students to advance cognitively. She could note that, while these skills are not easily transferable from one person to the next, they can be modelled by the professor who is willing to elaborate out loud to the class on the approaches that he or she has found successful – as long as that professor is careful to point out that this is only one way of thinking about a possible solution and that there may be many other valid approaches. Ann could be referred to published sources (for example, Baxter Margolda, 1992; Crow, 1989; Davidson and Worsham, 1992) that discuss cognitive development in prac-tical terms and/or provide examples of classroom activities that allow students to practise development of 'critical thinking' skills.

Ken expressed concerns related to a perceived mismatch between the student-centred nature of PBL and the notion of 'authentic' assessment. 'Authentic' refers to course assessment in which faculty members clearly state learning objectives to students, along with the strategies that will be used in each case to monitor student progress towards achieving them. If PBL is truly a student-centred process, how can 'authentic' assessment occur? If students know faculty members' objectives, will this knowledge be the sole driving force motivating their learning?

In addressing this concern, Sarah could distinguish between student-centred and student-driven learning. While PBL can be the former, it is not necessarily the latter, and cannot be in the traditional undergraduate context, where each course must fit within a larger curricular framework. Such an integration is difficult or impossible to achieve if students are the sole determinants of what will be learnt in a particular course. And, unless students are writing the PBL problems used in a course, the faculty member has already set limits on the learning objectives for the course by his or her choice of problems.

With regard to Ken, one of the more difficult tasks facing faculty developers is dealing with the local 'expert', whose ideas are often at odds with their own on a particular subject. While it is important to recognize the real contributions such a person can make to the workshop, it is equally important to be sure that the faculty developers' messages come across without dilution or confusion. Acknowledging the comments of the 'expert', while clarifying or qualifying them as appropriate to ensure that the desired points come across, helps to defuse such situations.

Finally, in faculty development workshops it is also not uncommon to encounter a participant who is gifted at directing the focus of the workshop to his or her current needs (which are sometimes only indirectly related to PBL), thus challenging the facilitation skills of the most experienced of presenters.

Clearly, a successful leader of faculty development workshops like the one described needs a happy blend of knowledge; skills in leadership, facilitation and management of people; insight; empathy – plus patience and optimism! Just as for skills in using PBL, we trust that such characteristics can be developed rather than being innate.

References

Anderson, R S and Speck, B W (eds) (1998) *Changing the Way We Grade Student Performance: Classroom assessment and the new learning paradigm*, New Directions for Teaching and Learning, no. 74, Jossey-Bass, San Francisco, CA

Angelo, T A and Cross, K P (1993) *Classroom Assessment Techniques: A handbook for college teachers*, Jossey-Bass, San Francisco, CA

Baxter Margolda, M B (1992) *Knowing and Reasoning in College: Gender-related patterns in students' intellectual development*, Jossey-Bass, San Francisco, CA

Crow, L W (ed) (1989) *Enhancing Critical Thinking in the Sciences*, National Science Teachers Association, Washington, DC

Davidson, N and Worsham, T (1992) *Enhancing Thinking Through Cooperative Learning*, Teachers College Press, New York

Rogers, G M and Sando, J K (eds) (1996) *Stepping Ahead: An assessment plan development guide*, Rose-Hulman Institute of Technology, Terre Haute, IN

CHAPTER 15

THE **STUDENTS** DID THAT?

Case reporter: David Taylor

Issues raised

This case study deals with the induction of sometimes reluctant faculty members and students into a new PBL curriculum. It highlights some difficulties and offers a novel solution.

Background

The University of Liverpool Medical School is over 100 years old and until 1996 delivered a very traditional five-year medical course. Like most of the medical courses in the United Kingdom, it was divided into two: a two-year intensive pre-clinical course followed by a three-year clinical course. Each year the intake has been around 200 students, but this is increasing to just over 300 by the end of 2001.

A new curriculum was implemented in 1996, focused on what students need to know to understand a series of cases introduced through problem-based learning (PBL), two to five lectures per week, and clinical- and communication-skills classes. The pre-clinical/clinical divide was abolished and a programme of early contact with patients was established.

PART 1

It was the early 1990s and our medical school was preparing to change its curriculum. Among the steps that we were going to take was the introduction of PBL. Although several of us on the task groups that were charged with developing ideas for the new curriculum had experience with the sorts of methods we were talking about, we felt that we needed more than simply 'home grown' expertise. So a number of us were sent for experience and training to other institutions. Groups visited Maastricht and McMaster medical schools and reported on their experiences and perceptions. After consideration of these reports:

- We elected to follow an approach based on the Maastricht model.
- We decided that a process of revolution was more likely to succeed than a process of evolution.
- We concluded that we were in a position to mount a large-scale training programme.

It was the decision to introduce a large-scale training course that led to one of the major dilemmas. Our first approach was to invite people in groups of 20 or so for one-day introductions to PBL. People who had experience and training in PBL at other universities led the sessions. After a number of these initial training sessions and then three specific sessions aimed at defining PBL, refining the tutor's role in PBL and dealing with dysfunctional groups, we had a cadre of interested, enthusiastic and more-or-less trained staff. Finally, we felt ready to let the prospective tutors loose on final-year (fifth-year) students, to hone their techniques.

And that was when the trouble started. For this advanced stage of faculty training, we set up a number of tutorials during the final year's 'reading weeks' (four months or so before final examinations). We promised the students that the cases would be of use to them in their preparation for finals. We reserved rooms and arranged for prospective tutors to come in – but rather less than half of the tutorials actually took place! Students felt that they were being used as 'guinea pigs' in a great experiment and that they could learn more if they simply stayed at home. That is precisely what many of them did. Staff were really frustrated at being 'dragged in' from their other commitments to take sessions that the students didn't even bother to attend. A typical reaction was: 'David, I've had to cancel a clinic to come to this. What's the point of wasting my time, especially as the students don't care? I'm interested in the ideas, but, really, why should I take time away from my work to do this "training"?'

What would your response be to the hail of criticism from both staff and students at the apparent waste of time?
What was the subtext, from the students' point of view?
What do you think should be done next?
How could the tutor training have been handled differently?

PART 2

After this debacle, we used somewhat less ambitious methods for training our staff. For example, we included short PBL sessions with prospective tutors acting as students in our lunchtime training programme (which also gave us the chance to try out a couple of case scenarios we had been considering).

We introduced PBL earlier in the course: in the fourth year on one of the hospital sites and on a voluntary basis for the third-year students. This was not solely to provide tutors with experience in tutoring. It was more to allow the third- and fourth-year students to obtain some of the benefits of the new style of education we were proposing to introduce later to a new cohort of students.

In October 1996 (after several years of preparation), we finally admitted the first cohort of students to our new curriculum. We introduced them to the principles of PBL, in writing and with a presentation. We then gave the students a short introductory module where we could focus on getting the technique of PBL established.

Many students were actively involved in the development and management of the new curriculum, and several of them came to the monthly training sessions that we ran for the PBL tutors. At least a few of the students were willing to express their opinions during the training sessions, and most of our tutors were pleased to hear what they had to say. However, there were also some tense moments!

On one memorable occasion, one of the students, Paul, commented: 'We think PBL is probably going to work, and we certainly enjoy the sessions. But I don't think my group are getting as much out of it as we could. We make lots of lists, but I think we are mostly missing out on the cross-linking of ideas, and we're really not getting very far with the non-scientific aspects of the cases. Another problem is that if we make lists, we tend to go down the lists looking for learning objectives.'

Before anyone else could say anything, Ann, another student, said: 'That makes it difficult to apply the learning objectives to the case, and it means that we often miss things if we didn't think of them in sequence. We feel that the sessions could go better. Would it be all right if we, the students, run a training session for you, the staff, to show you what we think would work?'

Well, what could we say in response to such a request?! We decided that, if we were serious about our course being student centred, we had no real choice.

A month later, the students led an excellent tutor training session. In it, they showed us how they would like to conduct their PBL sessions. They had come across the 'mind-map' technique, and a couple of groups had tried it out in previous tutorials. Ann, the student who had suggested the session, explained how mind-maps worked. Then the students divided the staff at the training session into small groups, and each student acted as a PBL tutor. This meant, of course, that we were forced to use the system ourselves on a case that the students had developed.

This tutor training session was a watershed in our implementation of PBL. The technique that was demonstrated proved popular, and most groups, with greater or lesser degrees of sophistication, now use it. Most importantly, it was a public demonstration that we regarded the students as being key movers in the new curriculum. They showed themselves and the rest of the medical school community that they were active and willing partners in the educational enterprise. For our part, we showed the students that we were prepared to learn from them and adopt their suggestions.

In the years since then, organizing and maintaining the course have become progressively more complex. The familiar traditional course has been replaced by the new curriculum as the cohort of students that entered in 1996 has moved through the programme. During 1999, we were faced with deciding how to teach the next new cohort of students about PBL. The original induction session had been swamped by other introductory talks, so we knew that something different had to happen. For various reasons, we had also lost the introductory module, where the students had been able to practise PBL without worrying unduly about the quality of the learning objectives. The course handbook was being rewritten, and the older written material about PBL that we had originally produced for the students bore little resemblance to the course we had developed.

Given the changed circumstances, what method(s) would you recommend for introducing the new students to PBL?

PART 3

We have always seen it as extremely important to involve the students in anything we do. So as a first step, with the help of some of our students, we took the material that had been used in the introductory presentation and turned it into a booklet that was issued to each of the first-year students on registration. This was relatively easily converted into a series of pages for the World Wide Web, which in turn could link to our Medical Student Society's Web pages on PBL (which are more irreverent than 'Faculty' would choose to be!). This approach had the advantages of allowing us to incorporate graphics and photographs and of giving the new students an introduction to the computer network.

Next, a group of second-year students took the very first plenary lecture of the first-year timetable and 'did' a PBL tutorial in front of all of the first-year students with me as the tutor. We used a specially written case that was topical, as it referred to a vaccination programme for meningitis. Again, although we were trying to get across the principles of PBL, there was a clear message in the case, and the questions that the second-year students discussed and identified as learning issues were the same sorts of questions that our new students were asking. For most students, the plenary was followed by a PBL session with their own tutor. They were able to discuss what they had just observed, before getting down to sorting out the ground rules for their new group. All in all, these steps proved to be most satisfactory replacements for our original introductory sessions.

How would you envisage involving students in helping to prepare teachers and other students for PBL at your own school?

CASE REPORTER'S DISCUSSION

At the heart of this case is the extremely important and valuable contribution that students can make to curricular change. We have been most successful in our efforts at reform when we have involved as many students (and staff) in the process as possible.

Our experience has been that all change is painful. For a major change in philosophy, such as that represented by PBL, there is no substitute for training and involvement. From the earliest days of our training programme, we included people who we knew would be very unlikely to be involved in the actual teaching, from research professors to hospital administrators. We did this because we knew that we had to influence the culture of the whole institution.

In hindsight, we could have tried to involve more of the students from the traditional curriculum in the original training process, both as participants and trainers. We had not anticipated that so many of the traditional students would be antagonistic, but perhaps we should have been aware of this possibility. For the most part, they had no 'ownership' of the process of change and had little interest in it. We had included them in the development teams and in many of the training sessions because we recognized the potential value of their involvement, but most of the traditional students felt that they were being used as 'guinea pigs' for the new course – which they would be missing out on – and consequently were being short-changed. In a sense they were correct, but only insofar as I believe that all students in conventional courses have always been short-changed. This is why, with considerable reluctance, we soon stopped using traditional students in tutor training groups.

The alternative – using prospective tutors themselves – had some advantages in that it actively inducted staff into the new teaching method and the curriculum itself. Once we had 'real, live' PBL-trained students on hand, we replaced this part of the training by observation of real groups, followed by the trainees taking real groups under supervision.

However, the best programme was developed only after we had the involvement of a group of students who *were* interested players: who had a real commitment and a real contribution to make. Since the course is supposedly student-centred, the students need to be visibly involved in the running and development of the course. Their involvement in showing staff and students how PBL is 'done' has been both enjoyable and effective.

The regular monthly tutor training sessions continue, although they are now roughly three-weekly. They provide social contact between staff and ensure that all of the tutors know what is happening and have access to the management team. We evaluate both staff and student performance in PBL. Both evaluation tools have been developed by students and staff together and provide plenty of food for our discussions. The whole exercise has left us with a course that is, I am convinced, a far more effective way of training a medical practitioner for a career of lifelong learning than was the old course. The same goes for the staff involved in the programme. Although many of us are now a little battle scarred, we are far more critical and aware of our teaching abilities. I know that I, and several of my colleagues, have found that this change has revitalized us and given us a new vision of what is possible.

The best part of the whole exercise, though, has been working with our students towards a common goal. And their contributions to helping solve the dilemmas described in this case study have been little short of brilliant.

ISSUES RELATING TO STUDENTS

CHAPTER 16

MATURE STUDENTS?

Case reporters: Emyr W Benbow and Ray F T McMahon

Issues raised

This case addresses the problem of dealing with dysfunctional groups in PBL, particularly ones in which a major source of the dysfunction is the influence of a few students who are older, or who have more varied life experiences, than the rest of the group's members.

Background

The University of Manchester is a large institution, in an urban setting, with about 18,000 students altogether. The Medical School has an annual intake of about 240 students, who mostly enter medical school immediately from secondary education at the age of 18 or 19 years. Some are older and will already have a primary degree in another discipline, or some equivalent experience, and in our terminology are designated 'mature'.

In 1992, it was decided that the previous course required a complete overhaul and that PBL would be introduced with the cohort that entered in 1994. Several other medical schools in the UK are now using PBL, but ours was the first to plan and implement such a radical overhaul.

PART 1

'I thought that these mature students were supposed to be assets to our PBL groups – and not a damn nuisance!'

'Bit of both, aren't they?'

Our paths had crossed in a dash from seminar room to laboratory, and we were discussing the PBL groups that we were sharing. We're both histopathologists, working in a department with a tradition of heavy involvement in medical undergraduate education. As well as participating in traditional didactic lectures, small group tutorials and practical demonstrations, we had both been closely involved with this medical school's first major, and successful, attempt to break away from the traditional undergraduate course. We'd helped replace a congested, dull, non-integrated lecture-based course with a managed course for our third-year students. In the new course, departmental contributions were integrated into a series of seminars on groups of common diseases, and individual contributions were tailored to a set of carefully constructed educational objectives. Presentations varied from five minutes to an hour, and all presentations were scrutinized by both peer and student review. It worked very well.

We had therefore been rather disturbed when we heard that the entirety of our medical undergraduate course was to be given over to a new form of teaching called PBL. As is often the way with these things, it took us quite a while to find out what PBL stood for. However, we recognized that, although the third year of the course was working well, much of the remainder was still rooted in archaic tradition and that a revolution was timely.

When PBL was about to start in our medical school, it was decided that staff facilitators would be chosen from its more experienced and enthusiastic teaching staff – and there aren't a lot of those in an environment dominated by basic biomedical research. We were both asked to take two groups of first-year students, each for three one-hour sessions per week for nine weeks. 'Expletive deleted!' we thought, 'we can't do that. It's completely incompatible with our clinical commitments.' We wanted to remain involved with this new venture, so we offered a solution that subsequently worked very well: we shared two groups and divided the facilitation sessions to suit our clinical workload. As it happens, our clinical interests are very similar, so it's relatively easy for one of us to do the facilitation while the other does the hospital work.

We had been pleased to meet our first two groups – and astounded how the average first-year student was so obviously younger, both physically and emotionally, than the third-year students we had usually taught. We arranged an introductory session, where the students were invited to tell each other, and us, about the special qualities they thought they might bring to the group. As we expected, most had entered university straight from secondary education, the typical situation in the UK. However, in Group A, two students stood out. Adam and Brendan were mature students: Adam was a qualified pharmacist, and Brendan already had a degree in electronic engineering – and they had very rapidly become firm friends. They were also both extroverts and spontaneously funny: the first few PBL sessions appeared to go very well. We thought this was great and expected the contributions of these mature students to be invaluable. Adam and Brendan picked up the important cues with consummate ease, and they rapidly wove intricate systems of links between these cues. We both like to think of ourselves as capable of the occasional use of humour, and facilitation often degenerated into an exchange of wisecracks with Adam and Brendan.

When other students contributed, it was usually to ask questions rather than to hazard possible solutions, and Adam's background in pharmacy enabled him to answer most queries. He was clearly a very bright student, and his solutions were almost always correct. At the end of each session, he and Brendan would rapidly summarize the progress they'd made, and they'd briskly assign learning objectives to the other students. However, we soon noticed that the remainder of the group was becoming increasingly passive. They'd perform the tasks that Adam and Brendan set them, but typically in a perfunctory and superficial manner: they clearly expected Adam and Brendan to sort out the significance of what they'd read. Although the group seemed to be lively, most of its students were learning very little. This clearly wasn't the way that PBL should work. All was not well.

Meanwhile, something very different was happening in Group B. Callum, another mature student, was the progeny of two headteachers, and it showed. He had a primary degree in Anglo-Indian studies, and observing him in the PBL group was like watching a well-meaning but impatient secondary school headmaster sort out a bunch of recalcitrant adolescents. He appointed himself chair in each session and briskly dispatched another student to the whiteboard to be scribe. He led the discussion by expressing his own views and came up with some spectacularly misguided hypotheses. We weren't bothered by the fact that many of his ideas were wrong – they were often creditable attempts to synthesize a solution to the problem under study – but we took exception to his total lack of tolerance of competing ideas from other students. These students were far less patient than Adam and Brendan's colleagues were. Naomi, in particular, repeatedly challenged Callum's overbearing style, but she got nowhere. She was hampered because Fiona, another member of the group, clearly disliked her and made little effort to disguise her loathing. Several other members of the group did little to help because they didn't want to seem to take sides in the standoff between Naomi and Fiona, and other students expressed their dissatisfaction by being rude to Callum, but he dealt with this with imperious put-downs.

Clearly there were problems with group dynamics and group functioning, and they seemed to be revolving around the mature students in both groups. What should we do?

If you were in our place, what would you do next?
How would you do it? Why?
What do you think actually happened?

PART 2

To deal with the problems, we first tried the few techniques that we knew about. One of us had been abroad on a course on PBL, based largely on role-play, and while it had been a salutary experience in all the things that could go wrong with PBL (though it hadn't anticipated the precise problem we had), it had been rather thin on solutions. We tried to encourage a more formal rotation of roles such as chair and scribe, we tried to engage less productive members of the group by asking their views directly, and we ended many of the sessions by asking our groups how they felt their PBL was progressing. They didn't seem to see there was a problem, let alone attempt to take possession of it. It was after a particularly frustrating session with one of these groups that we resolved to sort things out. We didn't think there was anyone else in the UK with sufficient experience of PBL to provide advice, so we tried a new idea of our own.

At this stage, PBL was very new in our medical school, and the course supervisor was still working on mechanisms for student appraisal. We had to make something up – and fast – and it had to be compatible with the fact that we had to cope with a large workload in the hospital. We decided to stage a series of interviews, one with each student, and we timetabled each interview for five minutes only. The interviews were structured and the students were asked about their perceptions of three main things:

1. how well they thought the group process was going;
2. how well they thought they themselves were performing as individuals;
3. how well they thought we were performing as facilitators.

For Group A, we expected very few criticisms: they clearly found their PBL sessions convivial. We had a vague plan to encourage the few students who weren't completely dominated by Adam and Brendan, but we were pleasantly surprised by the fact that most of them clearly recognized that there were problems with the group. Their views of the difficulties were very similar to ours. We explained that, if they wanted the dynamics of their group to change, they'd have to sort it out for themselves but that we would support them if Adam or Brendan responded with hostility to their attempts. Adam and Brendan had rather less insight into the group's difficulties, but both were very willing to listen to our views. We reminded them that PBL works best if each individual involved has to make an effort, but that we clearly recognized that they both had more knowledge and skills than the remaining students in the group. Indeed, we suggested, it would be more appropriate for them both to act as facilitators, and we explained the role of the facilitator to them. In particular, we emphasized the fact that the best facilitation is often the most unobtrusive and apparently passive. Both rapidly became superb facilitators, and there was no need for the members of the group to mount any active challenge to their position.

During his interview as a member of Group B, Callum was surprisingly constructive: he'd had no idea that what he was doing was counter-productive and he was willing to try to change. We explained the role of facil-itator and, as with Adam and Brendan, we suggested that he adopt a much more passive role. Naomi was also very receptive to our ideas and especially to our promise to provide support if her attempts to deal with Callum became fraught. The most difficult interview was with Fiona, who was consumed by her dislike of Naomi. However, she recognized the difficulty with Callum and, with some cajoling, she promised to put aside her dislike of Naomi in order to help deal with the greater problem. Callum was true to his word and he became a secondary facilitator, though he was clearly ill at ease, casting covert glances at whichever of us was in the room to ensure he had our approval. By the end of our time with this group, we felt that it functioned well as a PBL unit, but the previous frictions were never completely dispelled and there were occasional unfriendly jibes.

By coincidence, one of us became Callum's facilitator again in the third year of the course, though all the other students were new. He'd recovered much of his air of superiority, but the additional two years of experience that the other students had by this stage led to a very different outcome. This time, Amir led the main opposition. He didn't try direct challenges: he'd let Callum have his say, and he'd then quietly announce, 'That's fine, Callum; you can go and follow your personal study agenda, but the rest of us are going to follow ours.' Typically, Callum would come to subsequent meetings and make contributions that clearly revealed that he'd followed Amir's agenda. However, he never confessed that he might have been wrong.

What do you think of the outcome?
What other options might have been tried in dealing with the situations described?

CASE REPORTERS' DISCUSSION

Our medical school encourages the recruitment of mature students, with about 10 per cent of the annual intake typically having a primary degree. They are interviewed before acceptance, in advance of the standard interviews for students offered places on the basis of predicted examination results from secondary school. Mature students have additional knowledge, which is a potential resource in a medical school practising PBL, but, as we found, they can also cause problems because their levels of knowledge and experience are so much greater than those of the rest of the students.

When PBL started in this medical school, we knew that a lot could go wrong, but we had little idea about what to do when it did. There was a series of meetings where facilitators would discuss their problems, but these were dominated by individuals who were unsure about PBL and who wanted yet more advice and reassurance about the philosophy of this new educational approach. These meetings were, in practice, a support group for teachers grieving for a way of life that they were just beginning to understand would never return. Lacking guidelines, we chose to approach our problems with Adam, Brendan and Callum with a series of very short interviews for two main reasons: there were severe time constraints because of our clinical overload, and we hadn't managed to sort out the dysfunctional interactions by the usual group management techniques. We were gratified by the responses we got, but in retrospect our expectations may have been low because we just hadn't realized that, especially in Group A, the other group members also had misgivings about the group's progress.

We discussed with the facilitator group what we'd done, and mid-semester interviews with their groups are now recommended for all facilitators. We recognized that we had a problem, which our limited experience did not allow us to solve with our initial approaches to group work. We considered alternative strategies, including an open meeting to be attended by all group members and ourselves as facilitators, but we felt that this would have encountered the same difficulties as in the main PBL sessions. Another potential approach would have been to have individual interviews only with Adam and Brendan in the first group, and Callum, Fiona and Naomi in the second group. However, this would have prevented the other members of the groups from having input into a process that was intended to provide solutions for the group as a whole. By providing an opportunity for each individual to give his or her opinion on the group dynamics within a structured, time-limited interview, we gained tremendous insight into the reasons for group dysfunction. At the same time, we were able to provide our observations of individual student performance as a means of modifying behaviour within the group for the rest of the semester.

This worked very well with Adam and Brendan, but we were less comfortable with the outcome with Callum, though it was good that his group also functioned at an acceptable level by the time they'd finished with us. It was some comfort that the ratings we received from the students were the highest awarded to any facilitators that year. We did especially well in their evaluation of the attitude statement, 'my tutor(s) understand the group process', but we feel we came uncomfortably close to disaster. We still occasionally see Callum in the hospital's corridors, and our relationship with him is cordial. Indeed, we like him for his passion and commitment, but he clearly still has a considerable deficiency of interpersonal skills.

We already often use a system whereby the overall group (each of our groups consists of from 13 to 16 students) works as a single unit only at the beginning and end of each PBL session, and for the bulk of the time discusses the case as two sub-groups in the same room. Another possible solution to Callum's problem might have been to sub-divide the group in a manner engineered to minimize the friction, but this would have been a convoluted solution with limited hopes of success. Ultimately, it might become necessary to dismantle a group, but this would be a logistical nightmare in the middle of a semester.

The instances reported in our case (and others since then) suggest the importance of identifying potential strengths of individuals within a PBL group so that they can be used for the overall good of the group. As facilitators, we should be made aware by the faculty of the presence of mature students in our groups, but the roles that can be played by such individuals will often not become apparent until the group has met on several occasions. We have found the mid-semester individual interview to be a particularly useful way to moderate or reinforce their roles.

CHAPTER 17

To Admit or Not to Admit? That Is the Question...

Case reporters: Chuck Shuler and Alan Fincham

Issues raised

This case addresses the issues of selecting students for PBL programmes, reconciling differing views (especially among students) of the nature and goals of PBL, and dealing with dysfunctional PBL groups.

Background

The University of Southern California School of Dentistry (USCSD) was founded in 1897 and has a primary objective of preparing graduates to enter general dental practice. Until recently, USCSD had a traditional four-year dental curriculum and admitted about 130 students per year. In September 1995, a parallel PBL track was established with an additional 12 students per class. Dental students at USCSD are taught by 103 full-time and approximately 600 part-time faculty.

PART 1

Oh dear – was last year going to be a case of 'beginners' luck' or was this year an example of 'one bad apple in the lot'? Which class was atypical? And did the faculty have anything to do with what happened?

It was 1996 and we had established a 'pure' PBL programme as a parallel track in our School of Dentistry the previous year. Twelve more students were added to the student body and enrolled in the PBL parallel track in two groups of six. Because of a late start in implementing the programme in 1995, the students were selected from the waiting list for the traditional track. Selection for admission to the PBL track was based on completion of a Bachelor of Science or Bachelor of Arts degree with an acceptable grade point average (GPA), acceptable scores on the Dental Admissions Test (DAT), and some evidence of either research activity or experience in group learning, and possibly relevant life experience. The first 12 PBL track students were not significantly different from the students in the traditional track in GPAs or DAT scores, but the PBL students were slightly older.

The first year of the PBL programme went extremely well and the students rapidly adapted to learning in groups. Students and teachers identified similar objectives and the learning outcomes were excellent. Flushed with success and the thrill of achievement, we prepared to select a group of students for the second run of the PBL track. We decided to initiate the process early and to select both PBL and traditional track students at the same time. The process retained the same admissions criteria used for the first PBL class, but we tried to recruit students who were even more educationally accomplished prior to application for admission to dental school. The second PBL track class was a remarkably highly qualified group of students. Both their GPAs and their DAT scores were significantly higher than those of their traditional track peers, and they had graduated from some of the finest US universities, such as Berkeley, UCLA, Stanford and USC. We began the second year of the PBL programme with high levels of optimism that the PBL track would blossom.

Even as early as the first week of the semester, however, we saw that our new first-year class had a very different style of addressing a PBL case from its predecessor. At first, the group facilitators were encouraged that the students directly confronted content knowledge and application to a case and that they expected high levels of evidence in the analysis. There was a more adversarial style between the students in one of the two small groups than in the previous class, but this was deemed to be within the range of acceptable behaviours for PBL groups. Their questioning style was commonly aggressive and pointed. Often a negative critique was delivered when an individual was deemed unable to respond appropriately to a question. The competitive and adversarial group style was interpreted as reflecting the quality of the students and their drive to assimilate and understand content at the highest levels. The perception was that with time and familiarity the students would 'mellow out' and would value and respect the contributions of all the members of the group. Facilitators were encouraged to moderate the sessions and reduce the competitiveness of the groups. However, we were confident that we were observing merely a normal process of group adaptation to PBL, and certainly the students appeared to be mastering the content well. It was also seen as positive that some of the members of the group felt compelled to pursue all the learning objectives identified for a case (rather than just their own individual topics) and thus expand and accelerate the group's achievement even further.

Our initial optimism was quickly extinguished in the fifth week of the semester, during the third case to be considered by the new class. Early in one of the mentored sessions, three members of one of the groups (Janet, Rob and Shelley) were engaged in a typically adversarial exchange when, suddenly, Nick, a non-participant in this exchange, leapt up from the table, shouted 'I just can't stand this **** anymore' and rushed out of the room! Up to this point, Nick had been a productive participant in group sessions and had been viewed by facilitators as one of the stronger members of the group. He had not previously exhibited any outward signs of frustration with either the style of learning or the actions of his peers. The five other members of the group largely ignored Nick's action, and the level of aggressive confrontation regarding the topic under discussion actually increased. The last two students (Gene and Christina), who had not been involved in the exchange, withdrew from the process. Their body language clearly signalled their intention merely to tolerate the remaining time in the session while avoiding being subjected to the confrontational discussion. Nick did not return to the session. The facilitator was caught completely unawares and could do little more than maintain minimal order until the end of the session.

What do you think is happening here? What contributed to the situation?
If you were the group facilitator or the course convenor, what would you do now?
What do you think happened next?

PART 2

Later that same day, we held an ad hoc emergency meeting with all of the programme facilitators to discuss this wholly unanticipated event, to try to identify its cause and to develop a plan to help the group and the facilitator. (The next morning we learnt that Christina, one of the students who had stopped participating in the previous day's session, had demanded a transfer to the traditional track. The Dean granted the transfer without consulting the PBL faculty. There had been no contact with Nick, the student who had left the session, and attempts to reach him were unsuccessful.)

Faculty from the PBL programme suggested that the facilitator could assist the group and further demonstrate the PBL process by suspending further consideration of the case and asking the group to refocus on the 'problem' being experienced by their group. The intention was that, if the group members could identify the nature of their difficulties, they could begin to resolve them and eliminate the group's dysfunctional behaviour.

Richard, the group's facilitator, described the session at which this suggestion was carried out: 'Accusations and recriminations were flying around thick and fast. Nick was back and his first words were an accusation of

Shelley, Rob and Janet. "You people have been stealing the preparation I've done for these group meetings and then you present it to the group just to glorify yourselves in front of Richard." Shelley replied, "Well, if the quality of your work had been satisfactory, we wouldn't have to do it all ourselves." Janet jumped in with: "A couple of members of this group" (and she obviously meant Christina and Gene) "are so lazy and cut corners so much that the rest of us could learn more without their contributions".

'In trying to figure out why Rob, Shelley and Janet felt this way, I concluded that they felt superior because of their high entering GPAs and DAT scores and because they had graduated from prominent universities. I think Rob, Shelley and Janet believed that the level of science preparation by the other members of the group during their pre-dental years was so weak that it was compromising their educational progress, representing a handicap to the group. Anyhow, after all this, Nick was distraught and Gene tried to defend a position regarding the role of the group and the cooperative learning environment. But Shelley, Rob and Janet would have none of it: "We're going into specialty training after graduation from dental school and those residencies are highly competitive. We're not going to compromise our career goals just to make a few other students 'feel good' about learning material they should already have mastered."

'At that point, Nick, who in fact already had a Masters degree in a basic science, again rushed from the room. In response, Rob said: "Good riddance, we're better off without him."' Richard concluded: 'I was getting more and more frustrated. I tried to get the four students left in the room to develop a sense of group cohesion, but it was all to very little effect. They constantly interjected: "Let us do the case", and "We're ready to learn more, so let's go." What a mess!'

Are you surprised at the outcome so far? Why or why not?
What action(s) would you recommend now?

PART 3

Frustration continued among all the facilitators. They voiced concerns that perhaps similar attitudes had in fact existed in the first class, but, through naivety, the faculty had missed what were now perceived as potentially damaging events. The previous year's students were contacted and their first-year experiences compared to the current events. Nothing similar in the way of student behaviour or group dynamics could be identified during their first year. When asked what they thought was happening with the new first-year class, their typical reaction was, 'What did you expect; most of that group are jerks.'

In an attempt to deal with the dilemma, the administration hired an outside professional facilitator experienced in group dynamics to spend two days with the class to try to break down the barriers. Since he was from outside the programme, he would be able to avoid potential faculty/student problems. After one-and-a-half days, the professional facilitator came to the faculty, exasperated. He commented, 'I have worked with prison inmates entering parole programmes and have never seen a group of individuals less likely to function successfully as a group.' He identified three subsets of personalities/educational philosophies among the 11 students in the class (Christina never returned), and he believed that these differences were in some ways a root cause of the problems. He identified four students who were over-achieving Type A individuals who had entered the PBL track believing that it was an independent-study-type curriculum and thus they could learn entirely on their own. These Type A students felt that the group identified what needed to be learnt but after the identification stage, the group had only a small role in assisting their mastery of the material. A second subgroup of four students thought that PBL would let them 'focus' on topics and to a depth directly related to the practice of dentistry, thus allowing them to avoid learning material not relevant to a dentist in practice. The remaining three students all had substantial experience in group learning and valued the group process. This minority of students had selected PBL for reasons that the faculty considered appropriate and they were frustrated that a group learning environment did not exist. The professional group dynamics facilitator said that he had 'never worked so hard' for his money and that the best outcome that could be expected for this group of 11 students was 'peaceful coexistence'.

A gloom descended on the PBL faculty and there was reluctance to continue the programme if student recruitment was so unpredictable. The 11 students in the class were reorganized into two new groups that were structured to eliminate destructive interactions between individuals. All of the facilitators participated in several dysfunctional-group workshops presented by an authority in that area and worked to identify strategies to prevent the development of dysfunctional groups. Facilitators became very active in monitoring group dynamics and they intervened quickly and strongly at the first sign of adversarial behaviour. However, these were seen as merely emergency, temporary measures. In an attempt to find a long-term solution, we decided to review our admissions criteria and process, and to see whether an alternative strategy could be developed so that the engagement of students with the PBL process could be made more predictable.

Careful review of the report from the outside facilitator led to our concluding that the segregation of students into 'Independents', 'Slackers' and 'PBLers' doomed the class to difficulty with the pedagogy. In the second intake of students into the PBL track, the number of 'PBLers' was insufficient to maintain the group learning environment and influence the behaviour of the 'Independents' and the 'Slackers'. All facilitators were able to reliably assign each of the 11 students to one of these three groups based on their facilitating experiences. Hence it was decided that the admissions process needed a PBL component to allow observation of the candidate functioning in a group environment and determination of his or her pattern of interaction with the other members of a group.

The admissions process was modified to include a three-hour PBL session facilitated by one of the faculty, observed by another faculty member and videotaped for future reference. The participatory PBL session ended with a self- and peer-evaluation component that mirrored the process used with PBL groups in the parallel track. This three-hour PBL session followed a 30-minute presentation on the nature of the programme and the components of the PBL pedagogy. After this half-day experience, the students were given an opportunity to decide whether this type of pedagogy would be appropriate for their dental education by self-selecting for continued consideration for admission to the PBL track. The faculty then evaluated the admissions-process PBL session to determine which students would be excluded from further consideration on the basis of observed interpersonal behaviours that could compromise the PBL process. Students remaining under consideration were invited to return to observe a three-hour PBL session involving a matriculated group of students working with a facilitator and to discuss their experience with the current dental students working in the group.

Prospective students were encouraged to ask current students about the pros and cons of the PBL programme and the nature of learning in this type of pedagogy. The current students were subsequently polled about their experiences and impressions of each of the candidates who had self-selected for continued consideration and this information was supplied to the faculty admissions committee. Candidates with acceptable PBL group activity were invited back for individual interviews with several faculty and were asked to complete a learning styles inventory. All of the information was compiled and the PBL faculty met to recommend a priority list for offering admission to the remaining candidates. The first PBL parallel track students selected in this fashion matriculated in the autumn of 1997. Their admission profile was comparable to that of their traditional track peers at USC. The GPAs and DAT scores were slightly lower and the average age slightly higher for the PBL students, but neither difference was statistically significant.

Right from the outset, the class admitted in 1997 was comfortable with PBL and productive in their group learning. Their mastery of material has been excellent and their performance on the National Dental Board Examination Part I has surpassed that of both their traditional track peers and the previous PBL students. The fourth and fifth classes have been accepted into the PBL parallel track using the same admissions process and all the students have rapidly and productively adapted to the PBL learning style.

Although the admissions process we developed requires a greater investment of time than the old one, it has been easily justified by the superb PBL process and outcomes observed with the third, fourth and fifth classes.

The use of this admissions strategy has led to several interesting selections. Probably the most striking has been one student who had a perfect 4.0 GPA and the highest DAT score and had graduated from an internationally renowned university but who was triaged out by all faculty because of his group interaction during the 'PBL interview', where he exhibited behaviour disturbingly reminiscent of the PBL class admitted in 1996. Despite his outstanding undergraduate achievements – or perhaps because of them – he was unable to function productively in a group setting even when the activity was identified as a component for admission consideration.

So in answer to our initial question: fortunately, it does look as though this was a case of 'one bad apple' (or bunch of apples) in the lot, although our method of selecting the apples had a lot to do with what happened. We're much better at choosing good apples now!

What do you think of the outcome?
How well was the situation handled at each stage?
What other strategies and tactics might have been employed?
What lessons does this case hold for you, especially in terms of admissions, for your own use of PBL?

CASE REPORTERS' DISCUSSION

This case demonstrates the development of dysfunctional group behaviours resulting from differing perceptions by the students regarding the nature of a PBL programme. Without specific previous experience of PBL pedagogy, students developed personal impressions of the PBL process that were not commonly shared. These impressions of PBL were further modified by each student's past educational experience, which resulted in a vision of PBL based on reaching past levels of academic achievement. The progression of the case was thereafter subject to multiple perceptions of the process rather than a common shared understanding. PBL faculty eventually realized that insufficient time had been spent during the admissions process to familiarize students with the pedagogy and to select students most likely to succeed with this method of learning. Failure to adequately educate applicants before matriculation about PBL could not be corrected later on. Once the students had entered the course, their pursuit of the learning objectives and their commitment to successfully completing assessments compromised any attempts to educate them about the process of PBL or the nature of learning in a PBL curriculum.

The past traditional educational experiences of the students have a major impact on their transition to PBL pedagogy. Students who are 'super-successful' in a high-powered university must develop an incredible competitive drive and independent motivation to achieve. This achievement is reflected in the grades they receive and those grades become the outcome measure of their accomplishment. All other classmates thus represent competitors who must be overcome. Consequently, 'grades' become an important measure of 'self'. These 'super-successful' students appear to give up the most in their personal self-evaluation when accepting the group as the unit for progress and consequently they adapt more slowly to PBL. Thus the group process can be viewed as contrary to past experience and unless the group rapidly demonstrates utility to the accomplishment of the 'super-successful' students, those students will revert to past attitudes regarding the measure of achievement. Since student assessment in PBL includes as one component assessment of the student by the facilitator of the group, some students begin to 'perform' for the facilitator to demonstrate mastery of the material and (they hope) achieve a 'high grade'. These behaviours further divide the group, making students competitors rather than collaborators.

The understanding of the actual nature of the PBL process is extremely important prior to the matriculation of the students. The role and strength of the group is critical to demonstrating that students can accomplish their educational objectives. Initially, it was assumed that students would grasp the concept of PBL quite rapidly and that they would learn the pedagogy in the course of beginning the academic programme. In fact, the faculty had always assumed that the first two cases of the curriculum would be primarily a mechanism for helping develop the PBL learning process in each group and not solely for the development of content knowledge. This proved to be an overly optimistic assumption and consequently students enrolled in the PBL track with quite widely divergent ideas about the nature of a PBL process. The divergent opinions were not addressed in the admissions process with the first two classes because there were no criteria that could be used in student selection. The progression of learning from the curricular cases did not provide sufficient time for a convergence of the concepts of PBL as a learning process. Thus the recruitment of accomplished, opinionated students resulted in a rapid development of intra-group antagonisms that were refractory to outside intervention and contrary to the requirements of PBL pedagogy. Reflection on the incidents led to the conclusion that students were not adequately familiar with the nature of learning in PBL and that there might be specific student attitudes that are unacceptable for admission to a PBL programme.

The admissions process that was developed included an emphasis on increasing student awareness of the PBL pedagogy through personal experience and assessment of applicants' conduct in a PBL case session. This addition required more time in the review of candidates. However, it quickly identified students with negative group behaviours. The PBL session as part of the admissions process also placed all the students in the same relatively unfamiliar position and required them to participate in a group setting. Most applicants had prepared for a traditional interview. The PBL group experience quickly demanded of them personal involvement in the process of PBL. An important outcome from this experience was that some students self-selected to be removed from consideration for the PBL programme due to the different nature of the learning process. This was a specific intent of the faculty and in general the self-triage by students was consistent with faculty's assessments of students' participation in the PBL session. Thus only students well aware of the nature of the learning and with demonstrable capability of working in a group advanced to final consideration. The experience with three classes accepted by this process has proved that additional time committed to candidate review results in a major benefit for the entire programme.

This does not mean that PBL is applicable only to a subset of dental school applicants. Although we have not been able to test the hypothesis, we believe that all students benefited from the PBL experience and would have adapted to the pedagogy more easily following admission. Since very few applicants had any prior experience of PBL-type group learning, this component of the admissions process would have improved the understanding of the pedagogy by all participants. If all the students are aware of the goals of the PBL process, then success would be predicted in a group with a strong PBL identity. This also requires a strong commitment on the part of the students in the group to engage in frank and candid self- and peer-evaluation so that it is necessary prior to admission to include this experiential component. Investment in student preparation and understanding of PBL either during the admissions process or prior to admission has proved to be a very valuable component in the successful implementation of our PBL programme in dental education.

Finally, it is true that a selection process like the one described may preordain success of a small programme by 'weeding out' potentially difficult students – who would then miss out on the benefits of PBL in promoting cooperation and developing interpersonal and communication skills. We suggest that, if the admissions process continually emphasizes the nature of learning and the expectation of group participation, candidates will be made aware of what is expected of them and of any need to adapt. If students are admitted to the course having this awareness, unacceptable behaviours can be confronted and rooted out before they become entrenched. Peer- and self-evaluation can directly address students' behaviours and lead to modification where required. If students enter a PBL programme with insufficient awareness of its nature and of the expectations for their behaviour, it may be difficult to change behaviours while at the same time expecting students to achieve content mastery.

CHAPTER 18

WHY AREN'T THEY WORKING?

Case reporters: Diana Dolmans, Ineke Wolfhagen and Cees van der Vleuten

Issues raised

This case focuses on the issue of poorly functioning tutorial groups in PBL.

Background

The events described in this case took place at the Medical School of the University of Maastricht, the Netherlands, a medical school with almost 25 years of experience in PBL by the late 1990s. Two hundred new students enter the school each year. Students meet in tutorial groups twice a week for two hours. Each tutorial group comprises about 10 students and is guided by a faculty member acting as tutor.

PART 1

As educationalists, we didn't know whether to feel amused or frustrated, but it certainly was interesting observing what happened. It was all related to the students' reactions to the PBL tutorial group meetings. When students enter our Medical School and experience their first PBL tutorial group, most of them are enthusiastic about this way of learning. One advantage of PBL suggested by teaching staff is that the discussion in the group should make the students curious and should stimulate them to spend time on their studies. Many students mention that they feel obliged to spend time on their studies because other students in the tutorial group monitor their contributions. They worry about feeling uncomfortable in the group if they don't prepare for the tutorial meeting.

It was distressing, then, that during the late 1990s students at the

Maastricht Medical School increasingly started to complain about poorly functioning groups. Their positive expectations about the group experience were all too often not met and they were feeling extremely disappointed. The typical complaint ran something like: 'Several of my group-mates don't attend regularly – it's really annoying.' Although there were no formal data available on attendance at tutorials, teaching staff confirmed the increasing absenteeism. Group functioning suffered from lack of input resulting from student absences and the groups became less cohesive. The teachers decided that something had to be done.

Why do you think this problem developed?
What steps would you take to try to solve the problem?
What steps do you think the teachers actually took?
What do you think happened as a result?

PART 2

The solution to the problem seemed obvious and simple to the faculty: 'The group meetings are important and the students aren't attending, so let's make attendance compulsory.' Faculty decided that absence should be penalized and the penalty was built into the examination system. To be promoted to the next year, students did not require a pass in all courses. The new rule was that students whose attendance at tutorial meetings was inadequate would have to pass six out of seven courses during a year, while students whose attendance was satisfactory had to pass only five out of seven courses. This necessitated a definition of minimally acceptable attendance at tutorial sessions. Because faculty felt that a requirement to attend 100 per cent of the sessions would lead to too many students failing, they decided that students would be obliged to attend at least 80 per cent of the tutorial meetings. Tutors were asked to record student attendance at each meeting. These data were collected and used to decide whether a student had to pass five or six courses for promotion to the next year of the medical course.

Although this solution to the problem had seemed intuitive and obvious, the new requirement did not in fact lead to an improvement in the functioning of the tutorial groups. Most students did indeed attend at least 80 per cent of the tutorial group meetings, so there was an improvement in the attendance rate. However, the requirement of 80 per cent attendance led to many students deciding to skip the last two group meetings for each course (ie 20 per cent). In addition, staff found that some students attended the tutorial meetings but did not prepare well for them. As a consequence, they were present without being actively involved.

Why do you think that the actions taken led to such disappointing results?
What alternative actions could have been taken and why?
What should be done next?
What do you think actually happened next?

PART 3

Faculty members were disappointed that complaints about poorly performing tutorial groups did not decrease in number after the introduction of the 80 per cent attendance requirement. They discussed the problem again and decided that it had been the wrong solution. The attendance rule caused students to attend meetings without preparing well and prompted a lot of students to skip the last two meetings: requiring 80 per cent attendance suggests that absence from 20 per cent of the sessions is acceptable. Teaching staff argued that it would be better to ask students prior to the start of meetings of a tutorial group whether they would be willing to attend, the premise being that only motivated students would participate. Any student who signed up as a participant would be obliged to attend at least 80 per cent of the meetings. The idea was that those students who were inclined to miss many tutorial meetings would not sign up as participants, so that the students who did attend group meetings would be highly motivated and would participate well. It was decided that an experiment would be conducted in one course. Afterwards, the experiment would be evaluated and, if the experiences were positive, the idea would be implemented in all other courses.

What happened this time was that all students signed up to attend the tutorial meetings for the course in which the experiment was carried out. However, they still failed to prepare well for the meetings and the original problem remained unresolved. What is more, some students were absent even though they had subscribed, and some students were present but did not actively contribute to the tutorial group meetings. The experiment was not extended.

Are you surprised at the outcome? Why or why not?
What should be done next?
What do you think was done next?

PART 4

The staff once again analysed the problem of poorly functioning tutorial groups. They decided that it would be worthwhile to obtain a clearer picture of the extent of the problem. Since all students evaluate each problem-based course in the Maastricht Medical School, data were available about the functioning of the tutorial groups. At the end of each problem-based course, students are asked to rate the overall performance/productivity of their tutorial group on a scale of 1 to 10 (6 being 'adequate'; 10 being 'excellent'). The data from all courses across the four curriculum years showed that one out of every five tutorial groups was judged as functioning poorly. On the basis of these findings, faculty members decided that the problem of poorly functioning tutorial groups was a major one and that it demanded attention.

Questions were raised, however, about what features were displayed by a tutorial group that was judged as functioning poorly. Teachers argued that a tutorial group should have more value to students than individual study; otherwise, students might decide to skip meetings. If students did not prepare well for the tutorial group meeting, the quality of the discussion would suffer, and the meeting might then be judged as unproductive. Subsequently, faculty members decided that it would no longer be students' mere attendance at tutorial sessions but their actual participation in the tutorial group that would be rewarded in the examination system.

An instrument was developed to assess students' individual contributions in the tutorial group process. From this instrument, students were given feedback that was intended to contribute to improvement in their behaviour in the group. The instrument was used experimentally in a few courses and tutors were asked to assess the contributions of each individual member in the group. During the experimental stage, the scores on this instrument would not play any role in the formal assessment system. The instrument had to be tested for reliability, validity and acceptability to students and tutors before it could be used summatively.

Presently, the instrument has been developed but is used only to conduct experiments. The intention, however, is to use the instrument in a summative fashion in the future because faculty members believe it would otherwise have no positive influence on the functioning of tutorial groups. Initially, as educationalists we were enthusiastic about the change from assessing only students' attendance to assessing their actual participation. However, we have been disappointed that teaching staff believe that the instrument would contribute to improvement in the functioning of tutorial groups only if it is used in a summative fashion.

What do you think of the outcome thus far?
How well do you think the problem was handled? Why?
What alternative actions could have been taken in order to solve the problem?

CASE REPORTERS' DISCUSSION

In our opinion, the problem of poorly functioning tutorial groups was not well analysed initially. All too often staff tend to assume that students are not intrinsically motivated to spend time on their studies and therefore they need to be forced to attend tutorial meetings. The finding that one out of five tutorial groups at Maastricht was functioning poorly confirmed the teachers' ideas about students. This led to the introduction of solutions based upon common sense, such as obligatory tutorial group attendance, and other ad hoc decisions, such as a preliminary voluntary 'sign up' before the start of a course. In fact, the symptoms were being addressed rather than the causes of the problem.

Faculty members eventually realized that rewarding students' attendance instead of participation was not desirable and they decided to assess students' actual contributions, but they again made an error of judgement in our view. The mistake was in their insistence on the summative use of this assessment instrument rather than just its formative use. Instead of providing students with feedback from which they could learn how to improve their functioning in the tutorial group, teachers again chose a solution that forced students to exhibit extrinsically motivated behaviour that would lead to passing assessments. In this situation, students are coerced into displaying behaviours that would result in a 'satisfactory' rating by the tutor even if they had not prepared well. This might lead to tutorial group meetings with a high 'ritual' value, ie a situation in which all the steps are followed at a minimum level, but in which the issues discussed are not really connected with each other, because students have not prepared the materials in depth. The group process would become trivialized.

In our opinion, the solutions that were chosen to solve the problem of poorly functioning tutorial groups can be characterized as teacher-centred (eg obligatory attendance at tutorial groups, tutors assessing students' contributions) rather than student-centred. In a student-centred curriculum, as the problem-based one in Maastricht is supposed to be, we might have expected solutions that led to providing students with formative feedback in order to help them improve their functioning as group members. But, as already mentioned, even the instrument designed to assess students' individual contributions to the tutorial group and provide them with feedback about their behaviour in the group was to be used summatively. Formative self-evaluations or peer-evaluations would not only lead to students becoming more aware of their behaviour in the tutorial group, but such evaluations would also lead to appraisals of the functioning of the tutorial group as a whole.

Although initially we were surprised that the solutions chosen were 'teacher-centred' rather than 'student-centred', we soon realized that most staff have experienced only the teacher-centred model during their professional training. When confronted with disappointing findings such as poorly functioning tutorial groups, they not surprisingly try to solve the problem with solutions they are familiar with from their own experiences during their professional training. During that training they spent time on self-study only when being examined. From this experience they conclude that the examination system is the only force driving student learning.

What steps should have been taken? What advice could be given to try to solve the problem of poorly functioning tutorial groups? The first lesson to be learnt from this experience is that the problem of poorly functioning tutorial groups should be analysed in detail before solutions are decided upon. Why did some students not attend the tutorial group meetings? Was it just because they were not interested or because they did not prepare well? Or was the reason for not attending the meetings a perception that the meetings had no value beyond their own individual study? Did students get messages from the examination system that conflicted with those that the PBL programme intended? Were some tutors unable to deal with poorly functioning tutorial groups?

The second lesson to be learnt is that one should always look for evidence from educational research in helping to decide upon solutions. The topic of poorly functioning tutorial groups has not yet attracted the interest of researchers in PBL. Using our own problem-based curriculum, we conducted a study in which the main research question was: what makes students judge that a tutorial group is functioning well? In other words, which factors determine a tutorial group's performance or productivity? We used theoretical perspectives from research on cooperative learning to investigate the charac- teristics of poorly functioning tutorial groups. The research findings indicated that a tutorial group's level of performance is highly dependent on the quality of the interaction in the group (the ability of the students to explain to each other in their own words aspects of the subject matter; the ability of the students to link the topics studied to each other, etc). A low quality of inter- action leads to less motivated students, which implies that some students let others do the work. This subsequently results in the withdrawal of students who were initially motivated. Ultimately, this leads to a decline in group cohesion, less motivated students and a low quality of interactions. Finally, students may decide not to attend the tutorial group meetings any longer (see Dolmans *et al*, 1998). More research is needed to identify the factors that determine the quality of the interactions in the tutorial groups.

How can the results of this study help other teachers? We would recommend that an action plan be developed to include training for students and tutors in how to:

1. encourage high-quality interactions in the tutorial group;
2. evaluate the functioning of the tutorial group on a regular basis;
3. make use of self- and peer-evaluations in the tutorial group using some- thing like the instrument developed to assess students' contributions; and
4. deal with problems of group dynamics (Hitchcock and Anderson, 1997).

As a result of the training, students and tutors would be expected to have better skills to stimulate high-quality interactions in the tutorial group and to know how to deal with problems of group dynamics. The use of self- and peer-evaluations would then be expected to stimulate students to become better aware of their behaviour in the tutorial group, to take responsibility for their own learning and to reflect upon their own strengths and weaknesses in an ongoing manner. We are confident that this would contribute positively to the quality of performance of the tutorial groups.

Although they seemed initially to be so obvious, the solutions chosen to deal with the problem of poorly functioning tutorial groups at Maastricht have so far been disappointing. We are hopeful that, in the future, the right decisions will be made. In making such decisions, teaching staff should realize that problems that arise in a student-centred curriculum should be solved with solutions that are student-directed rather than teacher-directed and should be based upon in-depth analysis of the problem encountered. Currently, a group of staff members is developing plans to renew the curriculum. We hope they will also address issues related to further improvement of tutorial group functioning. And of course the effects of any solutions that are implemented should be evaluated.

References

Dolmans, D H J M, Wolfhagen, H A P and van der Vleuten, C P M (1998) 'Motivational and cognitive processes influencing tutorial groups', *Academic Medicine*, 73 (10, Suppl), pp S22–S24

Hitchcock, M A and Anderson, A S (1997) 'Dealing with dysfunctional tutorial groups', *Teaching and Learning in Medicine*, 9, pp 19–24

CHAPTER 19

I DON'T WANT TO BE A GROUPIE

Case reporters: David M Kaufman and Karen V Mann

Issues raised

This case study addresses the issue of dealing with a student who fails a PBL unit because of poor participation in the group. He is academically very capable but prefers to learn on his own. He intends to pursue a career in research rather than clinical practice and has to pass the remaining units to gain entry to a PhD programme.

Background

Dalhousie University is located in Halifax, Nova Scotia, Canada. The Faculty of Medicine was established in 1868 and serves Canada's three maritime provinces of Nova Scotia, New Brunswick and Prince Edward Island.

The medical school, which serves approximately 90 students in each of the four years of its MD curriculum, introduced a revised undergraduate medical curriculum in 1992. The revised curriculum comprises a series of five- to ten-week-long sequential units (eg Pharmacology, Human Body) in the first two years. Other units (eg Patient-Doctor, Population Health) run longitudinally, throughout the year. The new curriculum emphasizes tutorial learning, with groups of seven or eight students working with a faculty tutor for six hours weekly for periods of 8 to 10 weeks. While a few lectures (three to five per week) were retained, the main emphasis is on self-directed, learner-centred, interactive and cooperative learning. In order to successfully complete the course, students are required to pass both tutorial and content knowledge components of each unit.

PART 1

I had just finished signing some letters, in my capacity as Director of Medical Education, when there was a telephone call from Dr Robin Woods, Associate Dean of Research. He asked, 'Do you know John Lee? He's one of our brightest and most promising first-year medical students, but he's just failed the second unit of the PBL curriculum. And it's all because he was given a failing grade in his small-group tutorial. As you know, I never supported this aspect of our curriculum. His failure could jeopardize his entire career as a medical researcher, so we have to do something to improve his tutorial performance in the next unit. It's critical that he pass the rest of the units this year or he won't get into our PhD programme in Medical Science. We want him in that programme.'

'Okay, Robin, I'll see what I can do and I'll get back to you,' I responded encouragingly. This looked like an interesting challenge. I decided that, before I did anything else, I needed to get some background information, so I telephoned Dr Susan Wilson, the Associate Dean of Undergraduate Medical Education, and got permission to review John's file on a confidential basis. I saw that John's grade point average and Medical College Admission Test scores put him in the top 5 per cent of his class, and that his admissions interview score was average. However, as I was reviewing his end-of-unit tutorial assessment form, two comments caught my attention: 'Very quiet member of the group – doesn't always appear to be tuned-in' and 'Very rarely participates in group activities such as questioning, providing information, reading the case out loud, or going to the board.' For a PBL curriculum, where participation is important both for successful group function and for a satisfactory grade, this was worrying. I decided to look further. For the previous unit, John's mid-unit and final tutorial assessments were unremarkable, except for references to his quiet demeanour.

The tutor who gave John the failing grade for the just-completed unit was a senior faculty member who had twice tutored this unit. I telephoned him to discuss John's case, and he emphatically confirmed the comments made on the assessment form. However, I was horrified to learn that John had not been told during the unit, or at the written mid-unit evaluation, that his performance in tutorials was unsatisfactory and possibly at a failing level. Only one other student had failed a tutorial assessment in the two-year history of the curriculum. We had a problem on our hands, in more ways than one.

Now that I had the relevant information, I was ready to talk with John and offer some help. At the appointed time for our meeting, John came into my office and sat down. He appeared nervous and angry, and he opened the discussion by saying, 'Dr Woods told me to come and see you about my tutorial assessment. Everyone knows that tutorial assessments are biased, and my tutor didn't like me much. Besides, I proved that I learnt the stuff on the exam. So what's the problem?'

I sat back and thought: 'What would be the best way to respond?'

How would you go about managing the situation that has developed?
What could have been done differently to avoid the problem developing?
How would you respond to John's opening comments?

PART 2

I began by acknowledging John's feelings and affirming part of his viewpoint: 'I see your point, John. You have a right to be upset, and you're right about tutorial assessments being subjective.' I paused and hoped that my response would help John cool down a bit, because now I had to explain the Faculty's perspective. 'However, your grade represents the best judgement of your faculty tutor, who observed you three times a week for eight weeks. That's 24 times. I can't comment on whether your tutor liked you or not, but I can assure you that he failed you based on your performance and not your personality. Our students rarely fail tutorials, so I have to assume that you need to improve something. Since you can't appeal a failing grade in a tutorial, you do have a problem. You can't fail again this year or you'll have to repeat the year. My job is to work with you to ensure that you'll succeed.'

I wanted to get a bit more insight into how John saw things, so I asked him, 'How do you think you did in tutorials?' He explained that he was quiet by nature and that he always worked very hard on his own. He didn't see why he had to 'change the way I am'. He said, 'I learn best by reading and listening, and I was involved in the tutorials in my own way. I don't want to be a groupie. That isn't who I am.'

I described the rationale for the small-group tutorial process and told John that the PBL curriculum is designed to help him develop skills in communicating and working cooperatively with his peers. 'These are important skills for all future physicians,' I told him. He replied that he didn't plan to practise medicine; rather he intended to become a medical researcher. 'I've been conditionally accepted into the concurrent PhD programme in Medical Sciences, but I've got to pass the remaining units to obtain full acceptance.'

'I can see that you're not happy about this situation,' I told John. 'But these are not matters that relate only to education. Do you have any idea of the interpersonal and team nature of scientific research? It involves tasks such as project planning, collaborating, managing people, grant writing and serving on scientific panels.' I continued, 'I think we have bad news and good news to deal with. The bad news is that the current situation is "a given". It represents a non-negotiable requirement for you and can't be changed. Do you understand?' John nodded glumly. 'The good news,' I continued, 'is that I'm committed to supporting you. I hope that we can work together to improve your skills so that you pass the next unit. I've been training tutors and helping students for many years, so if you work seriously with me, I'm confident you'll succeed. But it's up to you.'

I reassured John that the PBL process should help him develop skills in learning to work with many different types of people, skills that would subsequently serve him well as a member of a research team. Convinced by my arguments or not, John agreed to work with me and asked, 'What do I need to do?'

What would you want John to do next?
What would you want to do next?

PART 3

I realized that I had to respect the confidentiality of John's case and not bias the assessment by his new tutor in the next unit. Otherwise, my disclosure could result in grounds for appeal if John failed his tutorial assessment again. I telephoned John's tutor and arranged to observe his group. This is a regular practice in the medical school, which has established a peer observation network, so there were no suspicions of 'a hidden agenda'. During the tutorial, my own observation confirmed that John's level of participation was unacceptably low.

Later the same day, I met again with John to discuss my observations from the tutorial. I suggested various behavioural changes he could make, such as acknowledging contributions of other group members by agreeing or disagreeing verbally; volunteering to read a new page out loud; volunteering to be a recorder on the flipchart or whiteboard; asking questions to clarify information presented; offering information or opinions more frequently; and presenting his learning issues in a more interactive manner. John explained that he was not quick at 'jumping in' when a question was asked, so I suggested that he speak with his tutor outside of the tutorial to ask for assistance. For example, John could give permission for his tutor to call on him occasionally to respond to questions. I strongly advised John to 'get involved'. 'Find ways to be a participant, not just an observer, in a way that's comfortable for you. Your comfort zone should expand as you practise this.' I agreed to meet him after each tutorial (Monday, Wednesday and Friday) during the next month to discuss his progress and to work on his skills.

John and I met as agreed, and I found that his confidence and attitude began to improve. His mid-unit tutorial assessment after four weeks was satisfactory, and we both agreed to continue to meet weekly until the end of the unit. John felt he had found a level of participation that was comfortable for him – that is, not overly active, but still satisfactory.

Two weeks before the end-of-unit assessment, I asked all 11 tutors at the weekly tutor meeting whether anyone in their groups was at risk of failing. I was greatly relieved to receive a negative response. John easily passed the unit, successfully completed the first year, and entered the PhD programme. I was able to give a positive report on the outcome when I eventually got back to Robin Woods.

What other options might there have been for dealing with this situation? What are the main lessons that can be learnt from this case?

CASE REPORTERS' DISCUSSION

This case raises broader issues than merely what to do on those rare occasions when a student fails a tutorial assessment. Most obvious is the question of whether it is critical that all students work to develop and acquire process skills in tutorials. A key assumption of PBL is that both the process and content of learning must be valued. The content is important for obvious reasons, but the PBL process is important also. The skills (eg in cooperative learning, self-assessment, self-directed learning and critical reasoning) and attitudes (eg about the importance of lifelong learning) that students should acquire from PBL will be essential throughout their lifetimes of medical practice. Furthermore, these skills and attitudes are just as important in the research context as in the clinical setting. Scientific research involves many activities that require communication and interpersonal skills. Examples include project planning, collaboration, grant writing, forming teams and managing research staff. This is also an issue for John's mentors and advisers in the research programme he wants to enter. Do they understand the value of the skills learnt in tutorials for work in the laboratory? Being able to clearly articulate one's ideas to colleagues and respond constructively to peers are skills that improve the reasoning process for all involved.

Obviously, another important assumption of PBL is that students can, and will, improve their interpersonal and communication skills as they learn to participate effectively as members of a team, although each student's personal style will be unique and consistent with his or her personality and comfort level. A PBL curriculum does not have to force each individual student into a preconceived mould (ie to become a 'groupie').

The case also raises the issues of the students' perceptions of the PBL process and its rationale, and the influence that faculty comments can have on students' valuing and perceptions. Many of our faculty and students hold beliefs about teaching and learning that are based on their own previous learning experiences, which for the most part have been more passive and individualistic than those required in a PBL curriculum.

In handling this case, the Director demonstrated sensitivity and excellent communication skills. By listening to John Lee's concerns and acknowledging his feelings, the Director established rapport early on. This was

followed by a clear and direct explanation of the 'non-negotiable requirements' of the situation. The Director then took the time to explain to John
the rationale and benefits of working on improving these skills. In this way,
John's intrinsic and extrinsic motivation were both activated. Of course, the
most important piece of the remediation process was the follow-through that
occurred. The observation, meetings, discussion and practice were all
essential to John's success.

Nevertheless, in critically reflecting on this incident, we can identify points
at which some action could have been taken that might have prevented or
alleviated the problem. For example, early diagnosis and intervention should
have been undertaken: John should have had feedback on his performance
mid-way through the unit and been offered some constructive suggestions
for improving his performance. The acquisition of the required skills would
not have occurred 'overnight', but starting on the process when the problem
arose would have resulted in a more educationally sound experience for John.

In a broader sense, continuing work needs to be done to help both faculty
and students understand curriculum changes, the rationale for them, and why
they are important. Although the majority of faculty accepted the philosophy
of the new curriculum and voted to approve the curriculum change, the
actual ramifications of the decision were often not felt until later. Faculty have
sometimes not considered how curriculum changes fit into their belief structures. In preparing faculty and students for a curriculum that is as different
from the traditional as is PBL, it is advisable that teachers be helped to
recognize: their own assumptions about effective teaching and learning; the
values that underlie those assumptions; the importance of making those
values explicit to themselves and to their learners; and that the values of other
faculty and of students may well be different from their own.

Enhanced communication about and understanding of curriculum change
would also provide an opportunity to bridge the gaps among educators,
researchers and clinicians by focusing on their common goals with regard to
communication, interpersonal and reasoning skills. The situation described in
the case offered an additional opportunity, which was not used, to more
actively involve the Associate Dean of Research in the process. This would
have started a dialogue that could perhaps have led to stronger commitment
from the research community to the curriculum.

Some specific lessons we have learnt from the case are as follows:

- Criteria and standards for assessment of performance (pass/fail) must
  be explicit, clear and consistent with the philosophy of PBL. Students
  must understand that these standards will be applied without exception
  but that support is available to help them in both the process of learning
  and the acquisition of an adequate knowledge base.
- Students need to understand the rationale for PBL right from their first
  week of medical school, and the message has to be reinforced

throughout the curriculum. This is particularly important for the assessment of students' tutorial performance, which could be viewed by some students as a subjective process, not to be taken seriously. While PBL curricula do not intend to make 'groupies' of their students, there may be 'hidden curriculum' messages that students perceive about 'how to behave' in tutorials. As well as clear and frequent explanations of and discussion about the process, we need to be conscious of both our intended and unintended messages.

- Incidents such as the one reported offer opportunities for learning for all concerned, rather than being just 'problems to be solved'. During a curriculum change process, there can be an inclination to focus on solving problems to minimize disruption and to defend the curriculum, rather than using these as opportunities for discussion and growth. Such growth is promoted by the fact that every incident is unique and there can be no set formula for approaching it. The individual situation and its unique features are important in considering each incident.
- Remediation of performance in the group is a process of learning new behaviours and skills rather than changing students' personalities. These behaviours and skills are specific and relatively easy to learn with practice. When students improve their group participation and learning skills, their self-efficacy will also improve, providing the basis for ongoing learning. Students can use their tutor or peers in the group as a resource to provide help and feedback, but a formal system should be in place to support the remediation process.

An important question to consider is whether this case could have been handled in other ways. Another approach could have involved peer support by one or more first-year students or by more senior (second-year) students. We believe that some excellent students in either of those classes could have achieved a similar result, with much less support needed from the Director. However, as this was a 'high stakes' case and the first of its kind to occur in our new PBL curriculum, it was probably handled in the most appropriate manner. At the same time, it must be recognized that supporting students in this manner places a high demand on resources. This solution would not work if there were many more students failing; alternative, less resource-intensive and more mainstream solutions would need to be developed.

Finally, it is worth thinking about other possible outcomes. The Director was able to help this student, resulting in a positive outcome to this case. But what if he or the student had failed again? How could the issue have been resolved? Would the PhD programme have to rethink its entry criteria? Is it legitimate for the medical undergraduate programme to stand by these standards for student performance in all situations?

CHAPTER 20

REFLECTING ON ASSESSMENT

Case reporter: Jan Lovie-Kitchin

Issues raised

This case study explores the issue of assessment of student performance in a PBL unit. It examines the choice of a method that assesses the knowledge learnt together with the learning process of PBL.

Background

The setting for this case study is the fourth (final) year of the Optometry course at the Queensland University of Technology. Class size is 30–40 students per year. In a course that is mainly taught by traditional methods, I have used PBL for the past 14 years in teaching the unit 'Vision Rehabilitation'. In the case, the quotes in italics are taken from students' comments over the past three years.

PART 1

As soon as I heard about PBL (in 1985), it grabbed me! PBL sounded exciting, different and fun and I could see its relevance to the clinical situation in which my students' learning had to be applied. I introduced it immediately (in 1986) into my unit in final-year Optometry, in which I teach the management of patients with low vision (LV) due to untreatable eye disease. Unlike patients with normal vision, for LV patients the 'solution' to their 'problems' could involve standard optometric care, but it also often requires input from other rehabilitation professionals, so students need to build on and broaden their current clinical knowledge. The unit is therefore ideal for a PBL approach.

The students work in small groups during one- or two-hour weekly classes, with most work being done between classes. During the semester, the students work through the management of a series of 'patients'. Each week, each group identifies and develops a set of questions that pairs of students research. By the following week, the students hand in a two-page summary to answer each of these questions; I give immediate (overnight), brief written feedback on these summaries. This feedback is usually expanded upon in discussion with the group in the next session. There is almost never any problem getting the students to do this work, but some students complain that marks are not awarded for it.

At the end of each 'patient case', each group presents its management of the patient for the whole class to discuss; there is a covert element of competition here. I give brief, oral feedback to the groups on their presentations but again this does not count towards their final assessment.

Right from the start, I also required the students to keep a 'logbook' to track their use of different resources, such as references to papers or books and names of people or organizations they had contacted in researching the information they required to manage their 'patients'. My intended purposes for the logbook were, first, to monitor the students' exposure to a variety of resources and, secondly, to provide an information resource for the students to use in the future. The logbook was handed in at the end of the semester and I gave feedback on its contents, but it was not graded. Over the years, the quality and quantity of information recorded in the logbooks deteriorated. I had to remind students constantly to fill it in during the semester and to hand it in at the end of the semester. The students wouldn't take the logbook seriously. I became quite frustrated – I thought I was providing them with an opportunity to develop a useful resource for the future, but they didn't see it that way, and all it gave me was aggravation!

To assess the unit I had always used short-answer questions and patient management problems (PMPs) in conventional written examinations. I persisted with this in the first year I introduced PBL but was quite dissatisfied with the students' answers to the questions. I realized that the traditional written exam was not appropriate – it did not give the students scope to demonstrate the depth of knowledge and understanding that I had seen them gain during the PBL course. In addition, the PBL sessions were complemented by concurrent practical (laboratory) classes and clinical experience. How did I know that they were synthesizing their different learning experiences and applying them in the clinical situation? (For that matter, how did I ever know?!)

There were some basic facts and calculations that I wanted to be sure students knew, but it seemed logical to me that the assessment should incorporate the management of another 'patient'. They should be able to use all the resources that they had used during the semester (which should have been recorded in their logbooks!), just as they would when they graduated as practising optometrists. So for the summative assessment, I decided to use, first, a mid-semester examination to check that the students had learnt the basic facts and could work through a small PMP. Secondly, two practical/laboratory reports were assessed during the semester. Finally, at the end of the semester, the students were given a simulated patient (a 'paper case') that was to be worked through in the same way as the other cases 'managed' during the semester, but it was assessed and graded individually. They had a week to hand it in. I dropped the end-of-semester written examination, so there were three components to the summative assessment: the mid-semester exam, practical reports and the end-of-semester 'paper case', with the latter being weighted highest (50 per cent).

I continued with my PBL unit in this way for some years. I was convinced that the students were learning more about the management of LV patients now than they had ever done with me lecturing to them. But how could I know that for sure and how could I demonstrate it? Over the years, I gradually became dissatisfied with the assessment that I was using. As educators, we have in recent years been asked to prove that we are doing a good job, not merely assert it. And we are being asked to teach and assess students' generic skills; for example, have they learnt how to learn, do they take responsibility for their own learning, are they prepared for lifelong learning? How did I know this was happening? How could I assess the students in my PBL course to reflect these different goals? I wasn't convinced that the assessment I was using did this much better than traditional examinations had. Besides, the students were asking for credit for in-course work. What should I do?

What would you do?
Can any principles and concepts be used to guide the search for improved assessment?
What changes in assessment do you think took place and what effect do you think they had?

PART 2

I felt I needed to change the assessment method, but how? Should I react to the students' requests for more continuous assessment? I had a selfish reason for not doing this – it would take more of my time – but I also couldn't see the need. I gave feedback on work that was well done. In fact, I showcased very good work in class and gave guidance to individuals or groups when further work was necessary. I didn't need assessment as the carrot (or is it the stick?) to get students to do the work, but how could I collect 'hard evidence' that they were learning?

The main impetus for the change that I did make in the assessment for my unit was the fact that the students wouldn't use the logbook in the way I had intended. As I was not giving marks for the logbook, the students perceived that

I didn't take it seriously – so why should they? And on reflection, if I was serious about ensuring that they had exposure to a sufficient variety of resources during the semester, what was the point of leaving it until the end of semester to check for that? It was too late then! If I believed the logbook was worthwhile, I needed to allocate marks to it and review it more than just once at the end of semester.

From my readings, I began to realize that the logbook, or journal as others called it, could also be used to address my other concerns about assessment for my PBL course. By asking students to reflect on their learning process through the use of a journal, I would make the assessment itself a learning tool and collect the 'evidence' I was after. The students would tell me what they had learnt and show me that they could build on this and apply it widely. So, three years ago, I upgraded the importance of the journal. I now require students to write a reflective journal that is used to provide both formative and summative assessment. I read each student's journal two or three times during the semester and give feedback to encourage more in-depth reflection. At the end of the semester I grade the journal; it now forms the major component of the assessment in my unit. At first the students don't like keeping a reflective journal, but by the end of the unit, most of them realize the value of it: *'I must admit having never kept a journal before, I thought (initially) that the idea was appalling. However, I have found it to be an extremely useful learning tool and reading back over it has helped me see how my ideas on certain subjects have changed.'*

My objectives for the journal for the students are: 'to encourage you to engage in self-reflection and self-assessment as one of the skills required for practising health professionals; to allow you to identify your learning processes and track your increasing competence; and to help you synthesize the learning from your PBL activities with your practical and clinical experiences.'

The criteria that I use to assess the journals and the grades awarded are detailed below. These are cumulative, ie to achieve a grade of 5 (Credit), the students must show good evidence of criteria a), b) and c) in the journal. To achieve a grade of 7 (High Distinction), strong evidence of all five criteria is required:

a. Description – accuracy of knowledge and description of facts, events and processes, with a focus on a wide range of topics, such as your own readings, in-class activities, group presentations, practical sessions, clinical experiences, other personal experiences, etc. (Grade 3–4)
b. Critical thinking – demonstrating abilities to analyse, synthesize and generalize information from a number of different sources. (Grade 4)
c. Personal exploration – depth of reflection; ability to explore and evaluate your own feelings and attitudes. (Grade 5)
d. Making connections – your evaluation of the various learning experiences and the extent to which you make connections between theoretical principles and your own experiences or observations of professional practice. (Grade 6)

e. Cyclical reflection – the extent of reflection on the process of learning that has occurred, ie the changes and development that have occurred in your learning in this unit during the semester. (Grade 7)

The reflective journals provide me with feedback about the students and their learning processes that I have not gained from other methods. The journal encourages students to engage in self-reflection and provides me with evidence that they do so. For example, it allows students to identify their learning processes and track their increasing competence and confidence: *'In the management of Case 3, I strongly feel that my performance and involvement in the group are much better compared with Cases 1 and 2. Other group members can accept my ideas and I can express my ideas. I remembered that every time in group discussion for other subjects I rarely said anything.'*

The journal gives indications that the students are learning to take responsibility for their own learning: *'I guess I feel as if I've learnt something for myself, which is actually a lot more rewarding personally than the feeling that can be left with other subjects. So I feel like I participated in what I learnt. Importantly, I think that the more you put in personally to a subject designed around problem-based learning, the more you get out of it.'*

It also suggests that they are prepared for lifelong learning: *'Keeping the journal was difficult for me in the beginning but over this period, I have found it to be a useful learning tool as I can reflect on the changes I've made and skills developed. I think I'll keep doing this so that areas of weakness can be identified by this process of reflection!'*

I believe the use of the reflective journal has been a resounding success. I have gradually increased the weighting of the journal in the assessment from 35 per cent in 1997 to 62.5 per cent in 2000. It is a pleasure to read most of the students' journals. I think I can say that for the first time in 20 years of teaching I enjoy doing the assessment!

Why do you think the reflective journal has become a successful form of assessment for this PBL unit?
As an assessment tool, in what ways does it embody the principles of good teaching?
What ideas can a reflective journal provide for other means of assessing PBL?
What areas of assessment, if any, are not addressed by a journal?
What potential problems are there in using reflective journals for assessment?

CASE REPORTER'S DISCUSSION

Assessment in any course is about understanding the process and outcomes of student learning, and understanding the students who have done the learning. The aim is to make both their learning and our teaching better (Ramsden,

1992). It has been stated many times that assessment plays a key role in the quality of student learning. If I may paraphrase Boud and Feletti (1991: 246), 'the assessment tail wags the learning dog'.

Assessment must be congruent with the goals of a course. Rarely will one method satisfy all educational goals. The concept of assessment for learning first and for grading second implies the use of a range of assessment methods. Feedback on learning is a primary task of all teaching, necessitating both formative and summative assessment; these should not be seen as rigidly separate. PBL is a serious attempt to match the context in which knowledge is learnt with the context in which it will be applied. In addition, the process of PBL incorporates many of the generic skills that students need to acquire. It is logical that the assessments in a PBL course should reflect these different goals.

In my PBL course I use a range of formative and summative assessments – some might say too many – with the reflective journal used for both. In my opinion, using a reflective journal as the major component of assessment is exactly congruent with the goals of PBL by assessing knowledge and attitudes and the learning process itself. In particular, it enables me to see if students are making connections between the PBL unit and their clinical experiences: *'It is very good and useful to have these case studies because it gets you thinking as to what you should do in a consultation with a patient who has low vision. Although, as I learnt from my patient on Monday, nothing can prepare you for the real thing!'* or *'I couldn't believe my luck when my LV patient, Mr R, presented. He had RP which I knew all about after managing Mr V (Case 2).'*

From the students' point of view, the reflective journal is an unknown at first, so they are wary and nervous about it, but they have never objected to doing it: *'To be honest, I've often thought it's been a bit of a bugger having to keep this journal. On sitting down to write, I've been wondering what I would have to write about. Usually though, I seem to end up writing too much. I think it's been really useful for me. It's made me think a lot more about my patients, why I'm doing things, and the consequences of my management.'*

As one student succinctly put it, the reflective journal is: *'Good – hard to start and equally hard to finish.'*

The significant weighting of the journal towards the final grade makes the students take it seriously and write entries regularly. It becomes a continuous, habit-forming task, with no final 'cram' at the end of semester: *'The journal hasn't been nearly as bothersome as I thought it was going to be. Simply writing down what you have seen and learnt over the past couple of days really isn't that taxing, and it does help to reinforce what you have just understood.'*

One potential problem of reflective journals is that students might write what they think the teacher 'wants' to see. Some of the quotes from students' journals used in this case study may give that appearance, but it must be realized that they are only small extracts of the students' reflections and are being looked at out of context. I have never experienced this phenomenon and believe that such behaviour could not be sustained over a whole semester. Unless there is supporting evidence from personal experiences or observations, generic statements of learning would not be acceptable.

Because there are only small numbers of students in Optometry classes, it is not too difficult for me to give reasonably regular feedback on the journal. The summative assessment is criterion-referenced, not norm-referenced, so students can be confident that they are assessed on their own work and that they are not competing with others. Paradoxically, despite the fact that I am assessing the journal, it enables direct, completely private communication between the students and me, in what seems for some students to be a safer, somewhat less threatening way than face-to-face communication. It has occasionally enabled me to help them solve problems with other students: *'I actually followed the advice you gave me last time I handed this in. I had a confrontation... so I told her what I thought she'd been doing. She could see where I was coming from and it was good to get it all out in the open. Hopefully things will be better now.'*

Assessment – like good teaching – is about many things at once: it should encourage interest, commitment and intellectual challenge, enhance student independence and responsibility, make the teacher's expectations unequivocal and show respect for our students as learning partners (Ramsden, 1992). I believe the journal has been successful because it has served these different purposes.

I have found the reflective journal to be a valuable and powerful tool, for both the students and myself. I have been humbled by how thoughtful and sensitive some students are in their writings. I will continue to use the journal as the main form of assessment in my PBL course, as I believe it incorporates and helps to assess the goals of PBL.

References

Boud, D and Feletti, G (eds) (1991) *The Challenge of Problem-Based Learning*, Kogan Page, London

Ramsden, P (1992) *Learning to Teach in Higher Education*, Routledge, London

CHAPTER 21

ASSESSABLE DAMAGE

Case reporters: Alex Forrest and Laurie Walsh

Issues raised

This case focuses on what appears to be loss of face by a student of non-English speaking background in front of her peer group at assessment time. The fundamental issue is the validity of assessment in PBL.

Background

The subject 'Anatomy of the Head and Neck' is a compulsory component of the second year of the Bachelor of Dental Science (BDSc) programme at the University of Queensland. Alex, the teacher who narrates the story, had 10 years of teaching experience at the time of the incident described.

PART 1

At the time this incident occurred, I was running 'Anatomy of the Head and Neck' in a PBL format for the first time after having presented it in a traditional didactic fashion for five years. There were 49 students in the class, divided into six groups by self-selection, each group comprising 5 to 12 students. Class contact consisted of twice-weekly PBL sessions, while the subject assessment included elements of peer- and self-assessment, together with problem-based viva assessment sessions. The peer- and self-assessment was worth 30 per cent of the overall assessment for the subject and was derived solely from the students' grading, without direct input from the tutor. Because there were many student groups and several tutors, the tutors found it difficult to gain sufficient exposure to all the students, and this affected oversight of the peer- and self-assessment process.

Students undertook the peer- and self-assessments individually, with reference to all students (including themselves) in their groups. The students had to justify by appropriate written comments all grades they awarded. The grades awarded by each student remained confidential to the student giving the grades and to the tutors, and all were returned to me as the senior tutor for aggregation into summative assessment grades. Each student received his or her own compiled summative grade along with the comments from other members of the group (anonymously).

In order to provide a degree of quality assurance for the assessment in this subject, we gave the students 'spot tests' relating to the problems they had encountered during their PBL sessions. These tests involved real-world tasks relating to the problems in a way that tested students' understanding rather than detailed knowledge. In the instance in question, the students had explored a peripheral paralysis of a nerve, and they were asked to write a letter to a hypothetical doctor explaining how they knew the problem was a peripheral one and not a condition involving the central nervous system. The 'grades' awarded by other students and tutors for these spot tests were compared with the grades awarded during the peer- and self-assessment process. In the few instances where major disparities were apparent, tutors could use this information to examine the student and the assessment process more closely, and thus to identify problems that arose. At no time were the spot tests used on their own for summative assessment.

Sessions were held during which I was able to interview each student individually and provide feedback on the assessments, on the student's performance and on any problems that were noted in the process. Each of these interviews was videotaped with the student's full knowledge for later analysis and referral.

The first summative peer- and self-assessment was run during the sixth week of the 13-week semester, with a spot test soon after that. During the same week, the first of the feedback interviews was held.

I can still recall Marcia, a student of non-English speaking background (Asian), entering the tutorial room allocated for the interviews. I began by congratulating her on a pass mark, a grade of 'satisfactory', which was a minimum passing grade. I then went on: 'Your peer- and self-assessments were very favourable, but your tutors felt that there were fundamental gaps in your understanding, and this was confirmed by your performance on the spot test. Overall, we thought that you couldn't be given a higher grade on the evidence, but we'd be happy to discuss the nature of the problem with the peer- and self-assessment process with you and with your group.' I then produced the spot test paper and began to go through it with Marcia to provide some targeted feedback and to encourage her.

As soon as we began the discussion, Marcia stood up and walked to the door. She appeared calm but stated firmly: 'I have no wish to discuss the assessment at all.' When I pointed out to her that feedback was a core feature of assessment, she became very upset and said, 'I won't listen to any discussion anyway.' She then requested that, if she were to be failed, she be failed *now*, so she would not have to continue paying HECS, the Australian government student fee for tertiary education.

I told her that she had not failed, nor was there any intention to fail her. I also pointed out that in comparison with the other students in her year, her performance did not merit a higher grade, as assessed by tutor observation of her PBL group performance and by the objective evidence of the spot test.

Marcia then became furious, and in spite of the fact that I invited her to discuss any and all aspects of the assessment process and outcome, she simply walked out the door!

What do you think Marcia's perception of the problem is?
What do you think the teacher might have done differently when talking with Marcia?
What would you have done next?
What do you think Alex actually did?

PART 2

I was bewildered by Marcia's apparent over-reaction and immediately reviewed her self-assessment and the assessments by her peers in the group. The singular feature of all the peer assessments in this group (and this was known before the feedback session) was that their comments about each other's knowledge and skills were exceedingly uncritical. The comments bore great similarities from student to student, and all students within the group routinely awarded all others the maximum marks. This strongly suggested to me that collusive marking was occurring. The group to which Marcia belonged had self-selected to be a large group (12 individuals) comprising people from a similar ethnic background, and they held themselves aloof from other members of the class.

During the rest of the interviews with the other students that same session, I could hardly stop thinking about the incident. Why did Marcia react so strongly? Could it be that she felt that she was being singled out from the group and would therefore lose face in front of them? How could she know about the grades within the group (which were supposed to be confidential to the student doing the grading) unless there had been group discussion on the issue?

Some 15 minutes after the abrupt end to the interview with Marcia (and coinciding with the end of an interview with another student from her group), the door of the interview room banged open. In full view of the video camera (which was recording the entire incident), Marcia stormed in with a form that she threw on the table. She demanded: 'Sign this so that I can withdraw from this subject.' As calmly as I could, I explained to her that she couldn't withdraw from the subject without withdrawing from the BDSc degree, since it was a compulsory subject. She wasn't prepared to listen and aggressively interrupted all attempts to explain the situation. By this time, other tutors were becoming aware that a problem was arising, and another tutor, Michael, came into the room and sat in on the discussion. It was becoming apparent to both of us that the problem that was being portrayed by the student had little resemblance to the reality of the situation and the real problems underlying it.

We both tried to talk with Marcia in a calm and friendly manner, in spite of the elevating level of abuse she hurled at us. With increasing belligerence she said: 'I'm not prepared to discuss this any further,' and she prevented any conversation by shouting down comments from either of us. Subsequently, she once again left in a tantrum, providing no further opportunity to discuss the issues with her.

I considered my options. I could refer Marcia to the Dean, but that would simply be passing the buck without solving the problem. I could wait until she calmed down and then attempt to initiate the discussion again. Or I could convene a large-group meeting with the entire class to discuss the issues raised by the incident in open forum. I was pretty certain that providing another opportunity for continuing the interview would result in a repeat performance. I was also convinced that the real problem underlying this performance was far deeper than it first appeared.

What do you think is the real nature of this problem?
What do you think should be done? What are the options?
What do you think Alex will do?

PART 3

I really couldn't let this incident lie unresolved. After all, the whole premise on which the subject was predicated was student participation in the processes of learning/teaching and assessment.

I decided to convene a meeting of the entire class and discuss the whole issue of assessment with no specific reference to this particular incident. I felt sure that Marcia herself would bring up the deeper issues. The session was videotaped explicitly for future reference.

In fact, when the whole-class meeting was held, Marcia did not directly bring up the main issues. Instead, she took the tack of stating that 'a 30 per cent mark for a spot test is too much'. I pointed out to her that the spot tests did not constitute a form of summative assessment; they were run as a quality control measure on the self- and peer-assessments. Together with the tutor assessments and the self- and peer-assessments, they were used to inform the final grade awarded, but they were not, of themselves, worth any percentage of any grade. Marcia appeared to adopt her argument as a form of defence and once again she became aggressive. Of the 49 people in the class, all but one (her boyfriend) became frustrated as they attempted to explain to her over a 40-minute session how the tests actually worked. By the end of the session, it was apparent that she and her boyfriend had become physically isolated from the rest of the class.

No reference was made to the fact that collusive marking within Marcia's group had been uncovered and that unrealistic group assessments underlay the situation. Alas, Marcia's performance was by far the weakest in her group, so the disparity was more obvious in her case than for the others. This raised some serious social issues, given the similar ethnic backgrounds of her group members.

At the end of the semester, both Marcia and her boyfriend failed the subject and were granted supplementary examinations. Through remedial one-to-one sessions both were able to finally achieve the criteria and were able to gain a pass for the subject at these examinations.

How do feel about the way in which Alex responded to this incident?
Would you have acted differently if you had been faced with the same situation? If so, why and in what way?
What are possible interpretations of the events described in this case?
What cultural issues do you think this incident raises with respect to assessment?
What actions might have avoided the emergence of this problem in the first place?

CASE REPORTERS' DISCUSSION

The issue in this case is clearly the validity of our approach to assessment in PBL and, in particular, the problem of collusive group assessment coupled with the ethnic background of the group members. When she was confronted with an objective element in assessment, Marcia realized that her weak performance had been identified. This would now be made public because she was already aware of her peer-assessment grades, which would not be reflected by the grade she received in the first formal assessment for the course. The effect may have been compounded by the large size of Marcia's group. Alex had decided to allow the groups to self-select, with instructions for group sizes to be no more than nine members. This particular group had isolated many (but not all) of the students from a similar ethnic background and was larger than any other group. Due to our inexperience, we decided to allow the group sizes and compositions to stand. As a result of incidents that arose, including the one reported here, we identified both self-selection and group size as problems and in future years imposed executive selection of group members.

Among some Asian groups, the concept of 'face', or the maintenance of one's visible integrity and status, is an extremely important social imperative, if not the most important one. Marcia felt that she would lose face before her peers as a result of her relatively poor assessment, and the collusive nature of the self- and peer-assessment in the group could now become visible to other class members. Marcia also presumably felt victimized on behalf of her group, because as the weakest performer in it, by a considerable margin, she displayed skills that were conspicuously low in comparison with others in the group.

The Asian ethnic background of this student, together with the guilt and other pressures that she felt, may have led to an over-reaction at the interview. This created a situation in which reasoned discussion could no longer occur. We had hoped that peer pressure could be brought to bear to help this student realize that her views on the assessment process lacked wide support among the student body. However, Marcia may also have felt that she was being blamed by other members of the group for exposing their 'system'. As a result, in the large-group session, her group appeared to abandon her and her supportive boyfriend. This created intolerable social pressures for Marcia and her boyfriend and may have been a decisive factor in their failure in this subject. In retrospect, it is apparent that this was the most likely outcome of the strategy, and perhaps the situation would have been better dealt with by gentle and continuous encouragement of this student, rather than by precipitation of a situation that clearly contributed to the failure of two students.

The idea of using spot tests to stimulate learning and to serve as 'quality control measures' for assessment was fundamentally flawed. It became clear very rapidly that the spot tests were examining things that were quite different from the other assessments. Students seemed to be more acutely aware of this than the staff. This feeling was summarized well by Marcia in her comment about the spot tests comprising 30 per cent of assessment. While the spot tests were used only to inform the assessments, students sometimes perceived that these were the 'real' assessments, which then drove the learning. In general, students were supportive of the spot tests, believing that they provided some degree of validation of the students' own assessments. It was decided to remove the spot tests in future years and substitute closer tutor supervision, group discussion and learning contracts within groups to solve the problem.

The 'collusive assessment' issue was in part due to the members of this particular group being able to effectively isolate themselves from contact with, and from the learning experiences of, other groups. To address this, we decided to make the tutor a fundamental part of the peer- and self-assessment programme. Since the tutor was closely involved with the group, it was appropriate that he or she also assess group members as peers. As soon as this 'external' influence was added, collusion vanished and was replaced by more honest, insightful assessment. Tutors were subsequently encouraged to have groups discuss their performance and that of individuals as part of each PBL session, and this helped familiarize students with the assessment criteria they had to meet, as well as acquainting them with the standards that applied to assessment against each criterion.

It was clear, therefore, that a number of different issues had conspired to create the situation to which Marcia found herself reacting so badly. Each of these issues was therefore identified and dealt with. Similar problems have not arisen since, indicating that the strategies we have adopted seem to have been successful.

From our experience with the incident reported in this case, we learnt lessons about the selection of group members, validity of assessment and socialization of students. These lessons have had a profound effect upon our practices ever since. It has become clear to us that student understanding of the purpose, method and outcome of assessment is crucial to its success.

CHAPTER 22

THEY JUST DON'T PULL THEIR WEIGHT

Case reporter: Don Woods

Issues raised

This case deals with the issue of individual accountability in small tutorless groups. A student complains that she is doing all the work. She says that others commit to present material but come ill prepared.

Background

PBL in Chemical Engineering at McMaster is an adaptation of the Medical School's format. Large classes are catered for by using tutorless groups and by giving the students extensive training in self-assessment, problem solving and team work. This form of PBL is used for parts of two required courses in an otherwise 'lecture-style' programme. The two required courses are a fourth-year course in 'Process Engineering and Economics' and, as reported here, a third-year course in 'Process Modelling'. The subject knowledge being learnt varies but is usually engineering economics, waste reduction, safety and environmental issues.

PART 1

The third-year course in Chemical Engineering that I teach includes six weeks (18 hours of class contact time) of small-group, self-directed, self-assessed PBL. I handle a class of 30 to 50 students and assign the students to groups of five or six. There are no tutors assigned to the groups because there is only one instructor. During the first two weeks, students are introduced to the skills and attitudes required for the course through a series of four one-and-a-half-hour workshops. The topics for the workshops are 1) what PBL is, why it is important for the students, and managing change; 2) problem-solving skills; 3) how to work effectively in groups; and 4) how to be an effective teacher.

To inform members of the group about their learning attitudes, styles and preferences, all students share with the other members of their group their results from a series of questionnaires about their attitudes toward and styles of learning (ie one instrument to explore the student's attitude about his or her role in learning, one indicating preference for theory versus worked examples and generalities versus details, and one exploring the student's predilection for learning by rote, searching for meaning, or working hard in the context of the published syllabus).

Following these introductory workshops, students cycle through three scheduled meetings for each of four sequential 'problem cases'. During the first meeting, the 'Goals Meeting', the students read the case, list the learning issues and have these validated by me. They contract to undertake the teaching responsibilities from the learning issues, with each person contracting to return and teach his or her topic. At the second meeting, the 'Teach Meeting', students teach each other the topics they have researched. Each student is given written feedback from everyone in the group about the quality of the 'teaching'. The final meeting is the 'Feedback Meeting', at which each group prepares a reasonable 'exam' question based on the case. Each group's question is given to another group to solve.

After each cycle of three sessions, each student writes a Reflective Report. The analysis includes the feedback sheets from the 'Teach Meeting', the example test question from the 'Feedback Meeting', the learning objectives, and a personal analysis of the strategies used to teach, any change in attitude about PBL and progress in the acquisition of lifelong learning skills.

I had already worked successfully with fourth-year students for six years using this method, but at the students' request I had moved some of the PBL material into a third-year class. This was the first time I had tried this approach with third-year students. Late in the week during which the students were working on their second case, there was a knock on my door. Maria, a conscientious B student in my third-year class asked, 'Can I see you for a moment about something that is bothering me about PBL?'

'Please come in and tell me about it', I encouraged.

Maria sat down and launched into her story: 'For the first case, everything seemed to go ok. Some of the teaching done by the others was only "fair", but I put that down to it being our first attempt at this new form. The second time around, everyone came to the "Teach Meeting". Although we had all contracted to prepare and distribute "teach notes", I was the only one with "teach notes" to distribute. I tried my best to teach them, but they didn't seem to be paying much attention. When it came their turn, they all did a lousy job of teaching. No notes. Very superficial. No worked examples.'

'I'm sorry to hear about that', I responded, but I was thinking: 'Oh, oh – here's a problem that's going to require some thought'.

What are the issues that are being raised?
What do you think the teacher should do next?

PART 2

Quickly, I thought through the range of issues that might pertain. Is Maria expecting too high a standard? Does she have a lousy group? Did I not give them enough pre-PBL training or was what I offered perhaps ineffective? Is the method of contracting insufficient to get a commitment from all? Are the others living up to the contract but Maria is expecting more? Are they ready for PBL? Are the students too comfortable with the 'lecture system' and really not ready for or unwilling to accept PBL? Is this an issue that will 'resolve itself' as the students become more familiar with PBL? Is the problem with Maria, with the others in her group, with trying to introduce PBL too early in the curriculum, with me and how I set it up? I concluded that it was time to get more information to help identify a root cause.

'Who are the other members of your group?', I asked.

' Jason, Brad, Margarite and Suzelle.'

This was a typical group with a mix of academic backgrounds and abilities. I concluded that it looked like a reasonable group.

'How do you feel about your group?', I asked Maria.

'I don't know Suzelle very well but she seems ok. I expected Jason to be a conscientious driving force in the group. The others are ok. But they're just not pulling their weight.'

'Did it seem to work out all right the first time?'

'Yes, but none of us knew what to expect. In hindsight, we probably didn't do a good job.'

I knew I could follow up on this, but on the face of it this seemed like a group that should work well. I wondered if it could be the contracting (from the 'Goals Meeting'), their understanding of the teaching task, the delivery in the 'Teach Meeting' or their general resistance to change. To check out some of these possibilities, I asked for their scores from the questionnaires. From these, it looked as though several of the students were less prepared in their attitudes for PBL than I had hoped and more wedded to rote learning than would be desirable, but the distribution of results was reasonable.

To check out the contracting, I wanted to hear what they did during the 'Goals Meeting':'Can you lead me through the "Goals Meeting" for the second case?'

'Brad was assigned to chair the meeting. He didn't circulate an agenda, although we all had an idea about what to do so that probably wasn't a big deal. We spent the first 20 minutes brainstorming the issues and prioritizing them. Then you checked them as 80 per cent complete and helped us to see the additional learning objectives we should include.'

'Yes, your group did a good job of identifying the learning issues. Then, how did you contract?'

'We checked over the list; each of us identified a topic to work on. We said that we would teach in much the same way as the last time. Each person then completed the feedback form about how the meeting went and gave it to Brad, and we left.'

I reminded her: 'The contract was the hunk of paper saying: "We the undersigned agree to meet our obligation to research, study and teach our assigned...". Everyone was expected to sign it to help meld the contract among group members. Also, you'll recall I suggested that each group discuss individual members' preferred way of learning and that each student prepare "teach notes" to be distributed to all members of the group. Did your group do any of that?'

'We did a bit of that at the first meeting. The discussion about teaching style was brief. We just had the completed list I showed you – except, of course, for Brad.'

'What about the "teach notes"?'

'The first time we did agree by everyone nodding heads. We didn't sign anything at either meeting'... pause... 'I'd really like to transfer to Tony's group. Everyone in that group brought "teach notes" to both meetings. I looked at them. They were good. I must get on the Dean's honour list this year to retain my scholarship. I may want to go to grad school. I really don't want to have my grades go down the drain because the others don't care. You have control over that, not me!'

What is your interpretation of the situation that has arisen?
What other questions would you have liked to ask?
What would you do next?
How would you respond to Maria's request to transfer to Tony's group?

PART 3

I realized that, although Maria thought there was a contract to provide 'teach notes', this contract did not seem to have been created or signed. The other members of her group appeared not to have the same expectations.

The students in her group, and probably in the others in the third year, were not as prepared for PBL as I had hoped they would be. Using data from the questionnaires that the students completed, I concluded that, in contrast to students who elected a PBL format, these students from a traditional curriculum still preferred to have the teacher 'lecture'. They did not want to take ownership of the learning process and were reluctant to use peers (and the teacher) as resources.

I decided that I should add more structure and individual accountability to the format and I should not directly interfere with group processing. I resolved to have a brief 'State of the PBL' talk with the class as a whole, during which I would:

- remind all the student groups of the elements critical to success: 'contracts' and 'teach notes'. Some examples from the fourth-year class would be posted to illustrate options. I would also remind them that these elements should be addressed in the Reflective Report;
- remind all the student groups of the implications of the attitude and learning preference data from the questionnaires and describe how this information could help them; and
- explain that I would try to help them by monitoring individuals' progress by having class ombudspersons and by creating a feedback form for peer- and self-rating about individual contributions to the team.

While these were steps I intended to take with the whole class, I also had to deal individually with Maria. I declined her request to be transferred to another group, telling her, 'One of the skills students need to develop is the ability to work with people who have styles different from their own. You will have to learn to deal positively with differences. You'll almost certainly need this skill when you're working as a professional.' I also discussed with her some steps she might take to be more assertive with her group in an attempt to get them to improve their teaching of each other. Maria then departed and I got down to work!

I gave my 'State of the PBL' talk and then developed methods for monitoring individuals' progress. First: ombudspersons. I asked the class to appoint four class representatives who would give me occasional feedback about how well the learning was progressing and offer suggestions for improvement. This worked extremely well. The representatives raised issues that were easy to explain, rationalize and change. Above all, the students felt that I was concerned about and aware of what was happening in class.

For individual accountability, I developed a form that listed a set of desired behaviours and criteria. Some of the elements included were leadership, cooperation, initiative, attitude, effort and individual assignments. The form included sample rating criteria. For example, for leadership a rating of 10 meant: provided direction and inspired others; 5: willing follower, took direction easily; and 0: frustrated the group, blocked progress and criticized others. Similar descriptors were given for each behaviour and criterion. Each student was to rate him or herself and all of the other members of the group. The rating forms were given directly to me and not seen by anyone else. From the data on these forms, I constructed tables that allowed me to see at a glance how the students rated themselves and each other.

.Once everyone realized that this form provided a measure of accountability, the members of Maria's group (and of the other groups) started to communicate better with each other and their performance improved. This particular self- and peer-rating form worked well. First, the scores were relatively consistent. The self-rankings were consistent with the peer-rankings and, for Maria's group, she was ranked first by each of the members. Secondly, just the fact that such rating forms were completed and the results seen by the tutor meant an improvement in individual accountability. Individuals could not get away with poor performance without receiving low ratings from their peers. The diligent workers felt satisfied that their displeasure with a peer's performance was reflected through their ratings that, in turn, were seen by the tutor.

I considered a number of options for sharing the data with the students or using them for 'marking' students. However, as time passed and no one asked about the results, I took no action. The information provided interesting benchmarks for me to see the team performance and the students knew that I knew about their performance. I think they no longer felt that they could hide in the group.

Maria saw me in the hall about three weeks later and reported that her group was really working well. I didn't ask her to elaborate so I don't know whether it was the result of the use of ombudspersons, her assertive statements and work within her group, my 'State of the PBL' address, the use of the rating form or the Reflective Report. Perhaps I should have asked her.

How do you feel about the way this situation was handled?
The students seem to have responded positively to the rating form by just knowing that the tutor saw the results. What would you have done with the results from the rating form?
What other ways might be used to improve individual accountability within tutorless groups?

CASE REPORTER'S DISCUSSION

The two key issues in this case are: how PBL can be used in large classes where individual student groups do not have a tutor, and what might be done to overcome uneven participation in groups.

Working with tutorless groups presents its own unique problems. In programmes where a tutor is available for each group, the tutor is trained in the skills of problem solving, group process, conflict resolution and sensitivity to how to teach. For tutorless groups, these skills must be developed in each group member. While there is insufficient space here to deal with this issue in detail, these are the steps that I have found important (Woods, 1994):

- Have sufficient workshop time 'upfront' to develop the students' confidence in their skills (Woods, 1999).

- Empower students with self-awareness of their preferred styles of learning and those of the peers in their group. I have chosen two questionnaires for this purpose: Jungian Typology (*Jungian Typology*, no date) and the deep versus surface learning style using the Lancaster Approaches to Studying Questionnaire (Ramsden, 1983). In addition, the Perry inventory (Perry, 1968) helps students understand the attitude shift expected in a PBL course and the role of the tutor.
- As revealed in the case, recruit ombudspeople right at the beginning to provide ongoing feedback about how well things are progressing.

Of greatest concern in this case, however, is the fact that uneven participation and lack of attendance are the top two major issues for tutorless groups (Woods *et al*, 1996). In groups with tutors, part of the role of the tutor is to create, from the beginning, a learning environment where students are both empowered with most of the elements in the learning process and are accountable to their peers and to the tutor. In this case study, it was only when Maria brought it to my attention that I faced the reality of students being able to hide in the group. Student performance and contributions need to be made visible to the tutor – especially when the tutor is not sitting with the group! What can be done?

The three options I considered all dealt with making individual contributions explicit and visible:

1. Learning contracts – Knowles (1975) advocates the use of learning contracts. For engineering students, I have found that most groups prefer to create their own contracts rather than use a prescribed version such as the one proposed by Knowles. The emphasis needs to be on the importance of the creation of the written contract. The contract can then be used as evidence in students' Reflective Reports or handed in separately as evidence of performance in the 'Goals Meeting'. I rejected the idea of having all groups hand in 'contracts' because my experience with final-year students suggested that different groups handle this process in different and imaginative ways.
2. Teach notes – I could have asked all groups to hand in their 'teach notes'. Teach notes or concept maps provide excellent evidence about the quality of the teaching provided by individual students in the 'Teach Meeting'. The notes can be used in the Reflective Reports, handed in to the tutor, marked by peers from other groups or put together as a set of notes from each cycle of PBL. This option would make each person accountable. However, I also rejected the idea of requiring the groups to submit the 'teach notes' because I believe that groups have to be able to decide on their own how best to handle the 'Teach Meetings'. I did not want to require them to create 'teach notes' just for a mark or just for me.

3. Self- and peer-rating form – I had success with this approach. I realized that the rating scales had to have descriptors for each criterion. The form was carefully designed. The student response was very encouraging and it was unnecessary to do anything more than collect and inspect the data to achieve the desired effect of increasing the accountability of individual students in the group.

An option implicit in this case study involved increasing Maria's assertiveness and encouraging her to bring the issue to the group. As a general principle, groups can be asked to create their own guidelines about how to handle potential problems before they occur. In this case study, Maria had to do it after the fact.

References

Jungian Typology (no date) Myers Briggs Type Inventory (MBTI), Consulting Psychologists Press, Palo Alto, CA

Knowles, M (1975) *Self-directed Learning*, Follett Publishing Company, Chicago, IL

Perry, W G Jr (1968) *Forms of Intellectual and Ethical Development in the College Years*, Holt Rinehart and Winston, New York

Ramsden, P (1983) *The Lancaster Approaches to Studying and Course Perceptions Questionnaire*, Educational Methods Unit, Oxford Polytechnic, Oxford, UK

Woods, D R (1994) *Problem-based Learning: How to gain the most from PBL*, Woods Publishing, Waterdown, ON, Canada

Woods, D R (1999) *Problem-based Learning: Resources to gain the most from PBL*, Woods Publishing, Waterdown, ON, Canada (partially available from the WWW at http://chemeng.mcmaster.ca/innov1.htm and click on PBL, Jan 2000)

Woods, D R, Duncan-Hewitt, W, Hall, F, Eyles, C and Hrymak, A N (1996) 'Tutored versus tutorless groups in PBL', *American Journal of Pharmaceutical Education*, **60**, pp 231–38

CONCLUSION

In conclusion, several important fundamental issues have surfaced repeatedly in the stories told in these case studies. Many of them could apply to other educational programmes or innovations. However, they are particularly relevant to PBL because of the:

- resistance of faculty and students to change as substantial as moving from a traditional curriculum to one that includes PBL;
- fear of loss of control and of the unknown;
- unfamiliarity of many faculty members and students with the principles and practices of PBL;
- intense scrutiny that PBL is subjected to in order to 'prove' that it works at least as well as traditional methods.

The collective experiences of the authors illustrate the pervasive and omnipresent barriers derived from fear of loss of control and fear of the unknown. This is particularly true when it comes to sharing with or transferring to students a portion of what has been the traditional power and responsibility of teachers, with respect to what to learn, when to learn it and how to use it. When PBL was successfully implemented, these barriers were overcome through insightful leadership, broad-based faculty 'buy in' and ownership, and recognition of the need for faculty and students to have sufficient time to learn from their own experiences by trial and error and make modifications that promote reflective adaptation to new learning/teaching methods.

LESSONS LEARNT

Leadership and sound governance are crucial in introducing and implementing PBL successfully

The significance of effective leadership and of sound governance was a feature of most of the case studies in Section 1. It would be no great exaggeration to suggest that without adequate and sustained attention to these issues, all others would be at great risk of becoming irrelevant. Formal leaders, those with identified administrative positions, can either accomplish a great deal or create obstacles and barriers to meaningful change. At one extreme, ineffective formal leadership was a major factor in dooming to failure a proposal to introduce PBL to a curriculum (*Forward from the Retreat*). Sometimes, curriculum innovators are informal leaders. They are faculty members who are respected, skilled, energetic and resilient in their educational and political abilities, but they may not hold official titles in the institution's administration. Such leaders were effective at a university where a neutral stance was taken by the dean, and yet PBL was introduced successfully (*Overcoming Obstacles*). In this case, other influential individuals and groups took on the leadership role. Another illustration is the creative 'win-win' solution found by negotiating for rewards other than money (*No Money Where Your Mouth Is*).

The importance of continuous and vigorous leadership, particularly during the early phase of implementation of PBL, is demonstrated by *Lost in the Mêlée* and by *Mixed Models and Mixed Messages,* where changes in the deanship and consequent decreased commitment to PBL led to failure to implement desired components of the intended programme (*Lost in the Mêlée*) or to insufficient administrative support for a departmental PBL programme within a curriculum in which other departments taught by more traditional methods (*Mixed Models and Mixed Messages*). *Into the Lion's Den* and *No Money Where Your Mouth Is* also illustrate some of the problems that can arise when insufficient resources are made available for PBL programmes. In the example of *No Money Where Your Mouth Is,* the potentially harmful influence of 'service' expectations of teaching staff is superimposed. Again, although it might appear obvious that leadership, political and resourcing issues are primary determinants of success, it is remarkable how often these areas are either ignored or given insufficient attention.

There is an absolute need for 'buy in' and ownership of a PBL curriculum by faculty and staff

Effective change is accomplished by faculty. The change process must be inclusive as it proceeds or it will simply disintegrate or become inefficient and wasteful. Therefore, there must be sufficient time and opportunity for the development of ownership among staff (particularly sceptics), time to try new methods and learn from experience, and time for faculty to develop their own modifications that can help to make the new curriculum theirs rather than merely an imposition or a transposition. Facilitating such a change process is one of the roles of leadership. Lack of a sense of ownership was a contributor to the difficulties reported in several of the cases (*Forward from the Retreat* and *Lost in the Mêlée*), while the successes reported in *Overcoming Obstacles* and in *Redesigning PBL: Resolving the Integration Problem* owe much to their faculties' sense of having developed their own programmes. *Come and See the Real Thing* and *But What if They Leave with Misinformation?* provide insight into how 'buy in' by faculty can be promoted. In the former case, live observation of an actual PBL session involving experienced, competent students and tutor was effective. In the latter, experience as a tutor with students in tutorial sessions was a strong persuader. This case also illustrates how valuable the conversion of a sceptical opinion leader can be to the promotion of change.

The importance of effective faculty development programmes in preparing staff for PBL is often underestimated, with negative consequences

Sustained faculty development programmes are crucial. In the early, pre-adoption phase such programmes may serve to lessen teachers' fears – but they may not, as witness *Faculty Development Workshops: A 'Challenge' of Problem-Based Learning?* and part of the programme described in *Come and See the Real Thing.* More importantly, after acceptance of PBL, effective faculty development programmes may provide opportunities for faculty to learn the new skills and behaviours required of them. Subsequently, positive experiences with PBL running well should allay teachers' concerns (*But What if They Leave with Misinformation?* and *The **Students** Did That?*). It is essential, however, that they be effective programmes, or misconceptions about the roles and responsibilities of teachers in a PBL programme like those reported in *Why Does the Department Have Professors if They Don't Teach?* may arise.

Once there is agreement to adopt PBL, teachers (and students) need adequate preparation and time for the change – in terms of their understanding of both the philosophy of the method and their expected roles and behaviours. While observation of PBL groups in action or occasional tutoring of such groups may lead to acceptance of PBL, they are unlikely on their own to make faculty adept at using the method. *Come and See the Real Thing* shows that even participation by faculty as students in a PBL exercise can raise questions and doubts that may not be successfully answered until faculty gain further experience. Also, collaboration with outside experts or employment of their ideas can help address faculty's misunderstanding of some of the key tenets of PBL (*Why Does the Department Have Professors if They Don't Teach?*) and/or lessen their anxieties about adapting to PBL (*Faculty Development Workshops: A 'Challenge' of Problem-Based Learning?*). Much thought and effort needs to be devoted to the introduction and induction procedures for staff in any implementation of PBL. It is worth noting significant contributions that students can make to the process. The collaboration between teachers and students in preparing and running successful teacher training sessions (reported in *The Students Did That?*) is a notable example.

That students also need preparation is shown by some of the incidents reported in *Mixed Models and Mixed Messages, Mature Students?, To Admit or Not to Admit? That Is the Question...* and *I Don't Want to Be a Groupie*. In each case, students' lack of understanding or acceptance of their expected behaviours led to difficulties. Here again, in at least two instances, collaboration between teachers and students led to positive outcomes (*The Students Did That?* and *They Just Don't Pull Their Weight*).

Effective communication and collaboration in preparing for the integrated approach utilized in PBL are essential but are more complex and demanding than in a more traditional curriculum

Effective communication and collaboration are axiomatic for any human progress. It would be difficult to imagine that there could be functional governance and a general feeling of 'ownership' among faculty in the absence of effective communication and collaboration. The cases reported in this book demonstrate these issues to be inseparable. Those who experienced difficulties with implementation of PBL because of problems with leadership or ownership also reported breakdowns of communication and/or collaboration (*Into the Lion's Den, Lost in the Mêlée, Mixed Models and Mixed Messages, Forward from the Retreat*). If effective communication and collaboration were present from the start (*Overcoming Obstacles*) or if they improved (*Into the Lion's Den, Mixed Models and Mixed Messages*), success was more likely.

Conflict and uncertainty about power and control related to teaching and learning will arise

How conflict is managed will be the measure of leadership and successful change. Students taking responsibility for their own learning is at the heart of the philosophy and the process of PBL. There can be substantial anxiety and concern experienced by some faculty as they recognize that they will have to turn over some control of the learning environment to students in PBL. This may be sufficient to frustrate successful implementation of PBL. In the example of *Forward from the Retreat*, the anxiety of faculty was one of the factors that prevented PBL from being adopted at all. Furthermore, *apparent* acceptance of the principles of PBL is no guarantee of their acceptance *in fact*. *Lost in the Mêlée* describes the problems experienced when faculty who supposedly accepted PBL failed to hand over some power and responsibility to students. Anxiety and concern among faculty were also evident in the success stories reported in *Come and See the Real Thing, But What if They*

Leave with Misinformation? and *Redesigning PBL: Resolving the Integration Problem.*

Assessment methods have to be consistent with how students are learning in PBL

As paraphrased in *Reflecting on Assessment*, 'the assessment tail wags the learning dog'. This is as true of PBL as it is of other curricula. However, assessment demands even more attention in PBL than in other curricula because of the complexity of group- and self-directed learning and the aforementioned concerns of faculty that lead to the close scrutiny accorded to PBL curricula. Faculty concerns about assessment are the focus of the difficulties experienced in *Faculty Development Workshops: A 'Challenge' of Problem-Based Learning?* In *Redesigning PBL: Resolving the Integration Problem, I Don't Want to Be a Groupie* and *Assessable Damage*, uncertainty and lack of clarity among teachers or students about assessment expectations and procedures led to predicaments derived directly from inadequate communication. Students' perceptions of assessment requirements led to their ignoring some important learning issues during their work with PBL cases in *Why Do They Ignore It? Reflecting on Assessment* demonstrates the sort of intensive thought that could well be put into assessment in PBL and provides an example of an assessment method (the logbook or reflective journal) that is congruent with the philosophy of PBL.

Self-, peer- and group-evaluation are key features of PBL. *Too Little, Too Late?*, *Mature Students?* and *They Just Don't Pull Their Weight* describe some of the benefits of effective evaluation. In these cases, the functioning of individual students and of whole groups was improved by providing adequate feedback where it had previously been deficient.

Dealing with dysfunctional groups or with individual problem students is a fundamental part of small-group PBL

As demonstrated in *Mature Students?, To Admit or Not to Admit? That Is the Question…*, *Why Aren't They Working?*, *I Don't Want to Be a Groupie, Assessable Damage* and *They Just Don't Pull Their Weight,* matters involving group dynamics or individual students' behaviour can *complicate* other fundamental dilemmas associated with PBL – even when they are not the main *cause* of those dilemmas. Finally, *Not More PBL* deals with the interesting issue of responding when students appear to outgrow or feel unchallenged and bored with 'regular' PBL.

Although PBL has been implemented mainly in areas associated with the professions, there is no reason to believe that its applicability is limited by anything more than the creative imagination of teachers and learners. The cases presented in this book cover a wide span of subject areas, from biological and natural sciences, through several of the health sciences, to architecture and engineering. Whatever the curriculum area or context in which you are working, we trust that your own reflection on the issues raised by the cases will be valuable to you in making implementation of PBL at your school successful and rewarding.

FURTHER READING

Alavi, C (1995) *Problem-Based Learning in a Health Sciences Curriculum*, Routledge, London

Albanese, M A and Mitchell, S (1993) 'Problem-based learning: a review of literature on its outcomes and implementation issues', *Academic Medicine*, **68**, pp 52–81

Barrows, H S (1985) *How to Design a Problem-Based Curriculum for the Preclinical Years*, Springer, New York

Barrows, H S (1986) 'A taxonomy of problem-based learning methods', *Medical Education*, **20**, pp 481–86

Barrows, H S (1992) *The Tutorial Process* (revised edn), Southern Illinois University School of Medicine, Springfield, IL

Barrows, H S (1994) *Practice-Based Learning: Problem-based learning applied to medical education*, Southern Illinois University School of Medicine, Springfield, IL

Barrows, H S and Tamblyn, R N (1980) *Problem-Based Learning: An approach to medical education*, Springer, New York

Bloom, S W (1989) 'The medical school as a social organization: the sources of resistance to change', *Medical Education*, **23**, pp 228–41 (A superb analysis of resistance to change in medical schools.)

Boud, D (ed) (1985) *Problem-Based Learning in Education for the Professions*, Higher Education Research and Development Society of Australasia, Sydney (Includes examples of PBL from a number of disciplines.)

Boud, D and Feletti, G I (eds) (1997) *The Challenge of Problem-Based Learning* (2nd edn), Kogan Page, London (Includes chapters on PBL in a variety of fields.)

Charlin, B, Mann, K and Hansen, P (1998) 'The many faces of problem-based learning: a framework for understanding and comparison', *Medical Teacher*, **20**, pp 323–30

Davis, M H and Harden, R M (1999) 'Problem-Based learning: a practical guide' (AMEE Medical Education Guide No. 15), *Medical Teacher*, **21**, pp 130–40

Evensen, D H and Hmelo, C E (2000) *Problem-Based Learning: A research perspective on learning interactions*, Lawrence Erlbaum Associates, Mahwah, NJ

Friedman, C P, de Bliek, R, Greer, D S, Mennin, S P, Norman, G R, Sheps, C G, Swanson, D B and Woodward, C A (1990) 'Charting the winds of change: evaluating innovative medical curricula', *Academic Medicine*, **65**, pp 8–14

Gronlund, N E (1998) *Assessment of Student Achievement* (6th edn), Allyn and Bacon, Boston, MA (Important reading for all faculty interested in student assessment.)

Harden, R M and Davis, M H (1998) 'The continuum of problem-based learning', *Medical Teacher*, **20**, pp 317–22

Heifetz, R A (1994) *Leadership without Easy Answers*, Belknap Press of Harvard University Press, Cambridge, MA (An excellent book on leadership, which is an important issue in making change.)

Journal of Dental Education (1998) **62** (9) (Entire September 1998 issue devoted to PBL in dental education.)

Kaufman, A (ed) (1985) *Implementing Problem-Based Medical Education: Lessons from successful innovations*, Springer, New York

Levine, A (1980) *Why Innovation Fails*, State University of New York Press, Albany, NY (The essential book on change in medical education.)

Maudsley, G (1999) 'Do we all mean the same thing by "problem-based learning"? A review of the concepts and a formulation of the ground rules', *Academic Medicine*, **74**, pp 178–85

Mennin, S P and Kalishman, S (eds) (1998) 'Issues and strategies for reform in medical education: lessons from eight medical schools', *Academic Medicine*, **73** (9, Supplement)

Mennin, S P and Kaufman, A (1989) 'The change process and medical education', *Medical Teacher*, **11**, pp 9–16

Mennin, S P and Krackov, S K (1998) 'Reflections of relevance, resistance, and reform in medical education', *Academic Medicine*, **73** (9, Supplement), pp S60–S64

Nendaz, M R and Tekian, A (1999) 'Assessment in problem-based learning medical schools: a literature review', *Teaching and Learning in Medicine*, **11**, pp 232–43

Norman, G R and Schmidt, H G (1992) 'The psychological basis of problem-based learning: a review of the evidence', *Academic Medicine*, **67**, pp 557–65

Rankin, J A (1999) *Handbook on Problem-Based Learning*, Forbes Custom Publishing, New York (Mostly a compilation of some key articles on PBL.)

Regehr, G and Norman, G R (1996) 'Issues in cognitive psychology: implications for professional education', *Academic Medicine*, **71**, pp 988–1001 (A sophisticated analysis of cognitive psychology, learning and PBL.)

Schmidt, H G (1993) 'Foundations of problem-based learning: some explanatory notes', *Medical Education*, **27**, pp 422–32

Schmidt, H G, Dauphinee, W D and Patel, V L (1987) 'Comparing the effects of problem-based and conventional curricula in an international sample', *Journal of Medical Education*, **62**, pp 305–15

Schmidt, H G and de Volder, M L (eds) (1984) *Tutorials in Problem-Based Learning: New directions in training for the health professions*, Van Gorcum, Assen, The Netherlands

Vernon, D T A and Blake, R L (1993) 'Does problem-based learning work? A meta-analysis of evaluative research', *Academic Medicine*, **68**, pp 550–63

Walton, H J and Matthews, M B (1989) 'Essentials of problem-based learning', *Medical Education*, **23**, pp 542–58

WHO (1993) Report of a WHO Study Group on Problem Solving Education for the Health Professions, *Increasing the Relevance of Education for Health Professionals*, WHO Technical Report Series 838, WHO, Geneva, Switzerland (A report that would be useful for schools in developing countries trying to figure out how to go about introducing relevant innovations in education. It has a section on community-based PBL.)

Wilkerson, L and Gijselaers, W H (eds) (1996) *Bringing Problem-Based Learning to Higher Education: Theory and practice*, New Directions for Teaching and Learning, no. 68, Jossey-Bass, San Francisco, CA (A series of papers discussing the use of PBL in a variety of fields in higher education.)

Index